SHOWHOUSES

signature designer styles

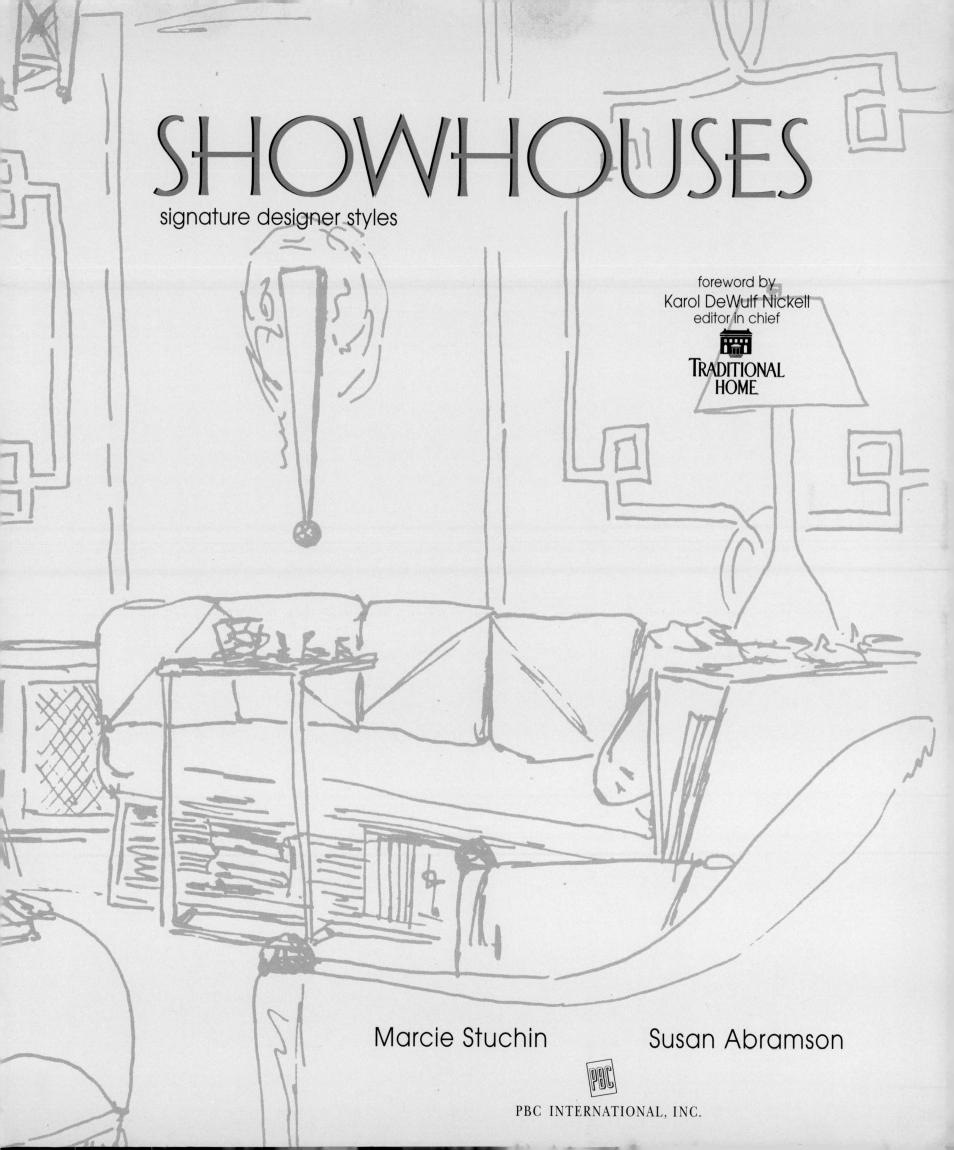

SHOWHOUSES

signature designer styles

foreword by
Karol DeWulf Nickell
editor in chief

TRADITIONAL HOME.

Marcie Stuchin   Susan Abramson

PBC INTERNATIONAL, INC.

*Distributor to the book trade in the United States
and Canada*
Rizzoli International Publications Inc.
through St. Martin's Press
175 Fifth Avenue
New York, NY 10010

*Distributor to the art trade in the United States
and Canada*
PBC International, Inc.
One School Street
Glen Cove, NY 11542

Distributor throughout the rest of the world
Hearst Books International
1350 Avenue of the Americas
New York, NY 10019

Library of Congress Cataloging-in-Publication Data
Stuchin, Marcie.
  Showhouses: signature designer styles /
  by Marcie Stuchin & Susan Abramson.
    p. cm.
  Includes index.
  ISBN 0-86636-594-X (Dom: hardbound). —
  l. Decorator showhouses — United States.
  2. Interior decoration — United States —
    History — 20th century.
  3. Decorator showhouses — Europe.
  4. Interior decoration — Europe — History — 20th century.
  l. Abramson, Susan. ll. Title.
NK2195.D43S78 1998   98-4661
747.213' 09' 045 — dc21   CIP

CAVEAT—Information in this text is believed accurate, and will
pose no problem for the student or casual reader. However,
the author was often constrained by information contained in
signed release forms, information that could have been in
error or not included at all. Any misinformation (or lack of information) is the result of failure in these attestations. The author
has done whatever is possible to insure accuracy.

10 9 8 7 6 5 4 3 2 1

Printed in Hong Kong

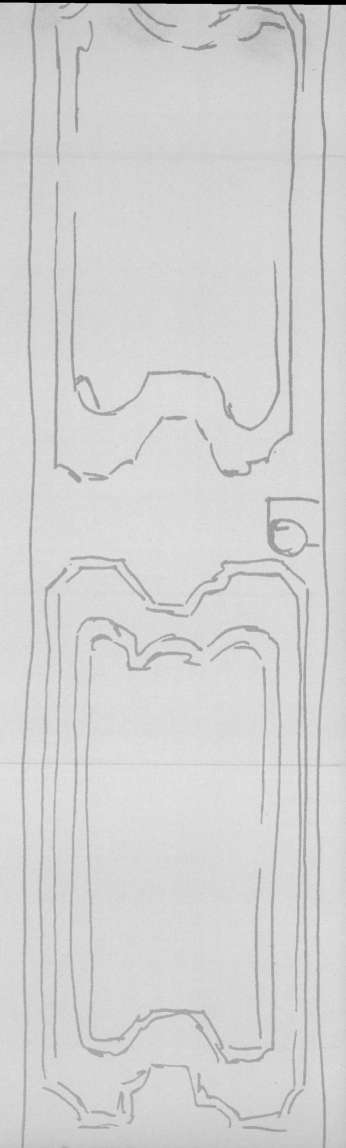

For Miles, Blake and Mallory,
who enrich my life with love,
laughter, and learning.

~Marcie

To my sons Danny and David,
who help put everything in perspective.

~Susan

CONTENTS

The designer showhouse is a great and uniquely American invention. Embodied by a single building but actually a multilayered entity, it brings together diverse ingredients of design innovation, community philanthropy and teamwork. Magic is born here, where almost overnight an empty structure blossoms into an exquisitely adorned home of designers' visions from top to bottom. Some of the very best ideas and trends from the world's top showhouses await you in this book—rooms of every style, size and mood imaginable are included. Whether or not you love every space shown in these pages, you will be rewarded with something very special—perhaps an idea for a fabulous color scheme or a way to decorate your teenager's bedroom. But most certainly, you will be inspired and entertained. So, enjoy these splendid visions and don't miss the opportunity to see a showhouse in your area or one that's open in a city you're visiting.

TRADITIONAL
HOME

Karol DeWulf Nickell
editor in chief

FOREWORD

Designer showhouses are the most eagerly anticipated fundraising events of the design community—stimulating and inspiring the creativity of all who come to view the astounding wealth of styles within their rooms. Held for the benefit of charitable community organizations, the showhouse serves as a design laboratory for the world's most celebrated designers and for those with careers on the rise. SHOWHOUSES signature designer styles is a bird's-eye view of practical solutions and imaginative settings within the liveable context of a veritable home. In this volume the best of these style-making interiors is preserved in its original splendor and vitality—offering a rich palette of creativity for every room. Meticulous preparation by committees, designers, artisans and suppliers yield fanciful spaces that, sadly, are gone within a matter of weeks. The images in this book continually inspire us and hopefully will do the same for you.

Marcie Stuchin   Susan Abramson

INTRODUCTION

A rich tapestry of design begins to form in the showhouse foyer, where a tone may be set for what is to come or a surprise may unfold. The foyer can reflect the elegant architectural style of the home or make a dazzling impression, commanding the visitor to stop and ponder before going on. To further the impact, designers create hallways as a canvas for transformation, seamlessly linking one room to another. Whether pairing a precious vase with a trompe l'oeil mural or combining styles and materials, showhouse designers use a unique vocabulary of elements to visually expand spaces which are often forgotten.

FOYERS & HALLWAYS

A passageway can be simple and serene, yet still have dramatic flair. Mark A. Polo of POLO M.A., INC. created a textured collage for the CRI • DESIGNER SHOW HOUSE in New York City, using a combination of rich fabrics, sculptural furnishings, and natural woods. He custom upholstered the walls in creamy silk, tailoring their seams with covered buttons for visual impact. PHOTOGRAPHY BY TIM LEE

ABOVE LEFT & ABOVE CENTER

A mundane service entrance in the 1920s' Tudor mansion presenting the PASADENA SHOWCASE HOUSE OF DESIGN in California, was transformed into a casual sunwashed passageway to the kitchen. Designer Kurt Cyr of KURT CYR INTERIOR DESIGN & DECORATION used a classic furniture arrangement for aesthetic balance. A sturdy informal console doubles as a work table, and holds baskets which provide storage for keys, note pads, and garden tools. The work surface is painted faux marble. Tumbled travertine pavers contribute to the manor house feel. PHOTOGRAPHY BY GREY CRAWFORD

ABOVE RIGHT & RIGHT

Patricia Bonis of PATRICIA BONIS INTERIORS, INC. designed an entry foyer to look like a Roman palazzo for the CRI • DESIGNER SHOW HOUSE in New York City. The light, spacious entryway was not always inviting. Bonis, in fact, removed all signs of heavy dark oak original to the flooring, wall paneling and ceiling. By paving the floor with yellow, gray and white limestone, and washing the walls in a soft golden color to resemble old distressed paneling, she immediately lightened up the room. A softly painted floral wall mural inspired by old Italian frescos circles the foyer. PHOTOGRAPHY BY TIM LEE

Designer Glenn Lawson of GLENN LAWSON, INC. renovated the grandly proportioned foyer of the HUDSON RIVER DESIGNER SHOWHOUSE in South Nyack, New York. Emphasizing its old-world appeal with a modernist sensibility, furnishings are spare and carefully edited. A richly carved chaise, center table and English cabinet, all from Florian Papp, set a refined tone. An unusual crystal chandelier echoes the openings of the pierced cornice. PHOTOGRAPHY BY LYNN MASSIMO

The residence which held the SHOWHOUSE AT THE SHORE in Ventnor, New Jersey, had a stately foyer and stairwell landing. Designer John Kelly of JOHN KELLY INTERIOR DESIGN, INC. complemented the architecture without making the space pretentious. A faux painted stone wall links the foyer and landing. Mindful of the wrought-iron stair rail, Kelly selected an antique iron chandelier. The existing stained-glass window is dressed with transparent fabrics to showcase the colorful design. PHOTOGRAPHY BY BARRY HALKIN

OPPOSITE

A grand staircase and elegant upper hallway set a formal tone for the entrance to the HOSPICE DESIGNER SHOWHOUSE in Westhampton, New York, designed by Marilyn Katz of MARILYN KATZ INTERIOR DESIGN LTD. Deep persimmon damask wallpaper, used throughout, provides a dramatic backdrop to a 19th-century romantic portrait and marble topped console table. PHOTOGRAPHY BY BILL ROTHSCHILD

LEFT & BELOW LEFT

An expansive trompe l'oeil sky is viewed through a faux wrought iron arcade, supporting a great skylight at MANSIONS IN MAY in Morristown, New Jersey. Designers Peter Cozzolino and Marguerite MacFarlane of THE STUDIO OF FINE AND DECORATIVE ARTS were inspired by the intricate vine-leafed balustrade on the grand staircase when they created their fanciful design. The upper walls, from the second floor to the crown molding, are painted in faux marble to repeat the pattern of the stone work below. PHOTOGRAPHY BY BILL ROTHSCHILD

BELOW CENTER

For the entrance hall to CASA F.O.A. in Buenos Aires, Argentina, Juan Alvarez Morales, Andres Levy, and Cynthia DeWinne of RETORNO ESTUDIO, painted the foyer walls in sunny South American colors. Stacked Chinese boxes, an 18th-century Flemish tapestry, and walnut plant pedestals make for an eye-catching montage. PHOTOGRAPHY BY ADELA ALDAMA

BELOW RIGHT

A golden oak staircase welcomes visitors to the CRI•DESIGNER SHOW HOUSE in New York City. Teri Seidman of TERI SEIDMAN INTERIORS gave importance to a small passageway by keeping its interest level high. A Regency bench echoes the border of a tobacco and brown floor covering. A painting by Susan Kahn provides a jolt of color. PHOTOGRAPHY BY TIM LEE

ABOVE LEFT

A stately Mediterranean house was the setting for the JUNIOR LEAGUE OF NEW ORLEANS DECORATORS' SHOW HOUSE VIII in Louisiana. Designer Kathy Slater of COLLECTIONS II continued a gracious feeling for the second floor landing by washing the walls in an old-world finish of ochre and pale yellow tones. A Louis XVI cane loveseat is filled with plush silk pillows.

PHOTOGRAPHY BY KERRI McCAFFETY

ABOVE CENTER

Myles Scott Harlan of MYLES SCOTT HARLAN INTERIOR DESIGN and decorative painter Douglas Wilson of DOUGLAS WILSON LTD. DECORATIVE PAINTING, gave prominence to the fourth floor landing of the AMERICAN HOSPITAL OF PARIS FRENCH DESIGNER SHOWHOUSE in New York City. They enlivened the space with Lucite, stainless steel, lacquered walls, and rice paper.   PHOTOGRAPHY BY PETER MARGONELLI

ABOVE RIGHT & RIGHT

A long and narrow hallway was endowed with charm by Rosalba Campitiello and William Johnson of EAST END INTERIORS for the MANSIONS & MILLIONAIRES DESIGNERS' SHOWCASE in Old Westbury, New York. Gilded mirrors and sconces, and crystal chandeliers allow this hall to shimmer with light.

PHOTOGRAPHY BY OLEG MARCH PHOTOGRAPHY

This vestibule became a colorful Moroccan tent once Richard A. Cannon and Richard P. Bullock of CANNON/ BULLOCK painted the walls and ceilings with North African colors. Presented by the DESIGN HOUSE in Los Angeles, California, the walls are faux painted to look like mosaic tiles. A sinuous wrought-iron console and wall sconce add to the exotic appeal.

PHOTOGRAPHY BY © CAMERON CAROTHERS PHOTOGRAPHY

ABOVE CENTER

This elevator alcove at MANSIONS IN MAY in Morristown, New Jersey, displays trompe l'oeil at its best. Morrene Jacobs and Joan Hamway of BLUE SKIES created a backdrop depicting Eloise, the famously spoiled little girl who lives at the Plaza Hotel. PHOTOGRAPHY BY MORRENE JACOBS

ABOVE RIGHT

The vestibule of the AMERICAN HOSPITAL OF PARIS FRENCH DESIGNER SHOWHOUSE in New York City, was refined by master gilder Hicham O. Ghandour of ANTIQUARIATO. The bench features antique gilding, while smoked glass wall panels with 22-karat gold leaf add depth. PHOTOGRAPHY BY ROBERT RIGGS

LEFT

An intimate corner of MANSIONS IN MAY in Bernardsville, New Jersey, designed by Gerald C. Tolomeo of GERALD C. TOLOMEO LTD., makes a strong statement with a pair of bronze ormolu lamps and a claw-foot Russian Empire console.

PHOTOGRAPHY BY BILL ROTHSCHILD

RIGHT

Flanked by a grand living room and rich wood paneled library, designer Michael Tyson Murphy of MICHAEL TYSON MURPHY STUDIO knew he had to create an equally impressive reception area for the AMERICAN HOSPITAL OF PARIS FRENCH DESIGNER SHOWHOUSE in New York City. He chose a neutral palette incorporating five shades of beige. A central trompe l'oeil niche appears as a limestone bas-relief sculpted wall with a 1930s' stylized floral motif. A glass Italian Art Deco table and Oushak carpet contribute to the elegant theme.   PHOTOGRAPHY BY ROBERT RIGGS

BELOW LEFT

In her entranceway to the stately home used for the JUNIOR LEAGUE OF BOSTON DECORATORS' SHOW HOUSE in Massachusetts, designer Beth Rodewig of RODEWIG RE-DECORATING/DECORATIVE PAINTING AND DETAILS wanted to play up the old-world appeal of the house. She achieved her goal using strong decorative objects and golden color complementary to the foyer's rich walnut paneling. A fleur-de-lis motif is repeated on wall stenciling and by the cast-iron finial.   PHOTOGRAPHY BY PETER JAQUITH PHOTOGRAPHY

BELOW RIGHT & OPPOSITE

To set the tone for the CASTILLO DE ARENA DESIGNER SHOWHOUSE in Fort Lauderdale, Florida, Lynne Herman of LYNNE HERMAN INTERIORS designed the entrance foyer to enhance the Mediterranean spirit of the home. She created a European villa with a trompe l'oeil mural that enveloped the space. A large scale demi-lune chest faces a massive wood front door.   PHOTOGRAPHY BY © IMAGE/DENNIS KRUKOWSKI

ABOVE LEFT & ABOVE CENTER

A pastoral triptych mural is the main focus of an upstairs landing in the entrance hallway at the MANSIONS & MILLIONAIRES DESIGNERS' SHOWCASE in North Hills, New York. Loraine Volz of IMAGINATION UNLIMITED enhanced the space with trompe l'oeil limestone blocks and a chair rail of faux marble slabs.

PHOTOGRAPHY BY MARK SAMU PHOTOGRAPHY & TIM EBERT PHOTOGRAPHY

ABOVE RIIGHT

Decorative painter Wylene Commander of WYLENE COMMANDER ARTS & DECORATIONS was given the task of transforming a small nondescript elevator cab in the townhouse which served as the CRI • DESIGNER SHOW HOUSE in New York City, into a romantic vehicle of transport. She painted the entire cab in a five process faux bois finish to look like aged burl walnut. Seascapes, ripe with symbolism, were painted on the upper panels to expand the space visually. The ash floor was given a marquetry pattern resembling a compass.

PHOTOGRAPHY BY © DANIEL EIFERT

RIGHT

Within the Carriage House of the OAK & IVY SHOW HOUSE AND GARDEN in Montclair, New Jersey, Carol Huber's ARTISTIC DESIGNS brought the outdoors into a drab garage. She created a fantasy potting shed by painting murals on the original walls and covering the floor with a trompe l'oeil cloth.

PHOTOGRAPHY BY © IMAGE/DENNIS KRUKOWSKI

Interior designer and muralist Joel Allen of JOEL ALLEN knew his mural for the thirty-foot-long landing at the KIPS BAY BOYS & GIRLS CLUB DECORATOR SHOW HOUSE in New York City would be viewed at close range by thousands. His Chinese inspired painting, awash in muted tones of purple, pink, peach, green, and blue, was intended to be elegant and uplifting. To draw the eye upwards, the artist perched figures on an elevated bamboo walkway. Its columns rise to ceiling height, visually expanding the space. Romance, natural beauty and music are central themes. A child playfully rides a tortoise for a whimsical touch.   PHOTOGRAPHY BY PIETER ESTERSOHN/LA CHAPELLE LTD.

NEXT SPREAD

Designer Anthony Antine of ANTINE ASSOCIATES, INC. glazed the walls of an otherwise dark entry hall in the KIPS BAY BOYS & GIRLS CLUB DECORATOR SHOW HOUSE in New York City with a sunny yellow color to liven up the space. Fine English antiques, including a Regency-style desk and ebonized console add a touch of glamour.   PHOTOGRAPHY BY PETER PAIGE

Living rooms are center stage at a showhouse, providing the greatest opportunity for a designer to experiment creatively without limitations or client requirements. New styles often evolve here, where the combination of color, texture, personality, scale, light and function creates a dramatic and powerful backdrop for the showhouse. These rooms can be both public spaces and private areas—havens for conversation, entertainment and family gatherings. Like living rooms, sitting rooms may also offer a more intimate oasis, where narratives about the personalities who inhabit them are conveyed through the unique embodiment of the designer's own vision.

LIVING & SITTING ROOMS

PREVIOUS SPREAD

Assigned the high ceilinged, stately living room for MANSIONS IN MAY in Morristown, New Jersey, Anne Cooper of ANNE COOPER INTERIORS, INC. opted to re-create a luxurious sun-drenched grand salon inspired by villas in the South of France. She draped the towering windows with luxurious fabrics in Mediterranean blue. A couch is swathed in sea-foam green. The European armoire, chandelier and coffee table are all from Goralnick ∗ Buchanan A & D, Inc. Behind impressive iron gates, the designer commissioned an imaginary terrace view overlooking an azure sea. Regal European chairs are covered with patterned slipcovers which make them appear more casual. PHOTOGRAPHY BY © PHILLIP ENNIS

ABOVE LEFT & RIGHT

For the ROGERS MEMORIAL LIBRARY DESIGNERS' SHOWHOUSE in Southampton, New York, designers Billy W. Francis and Ed Russell of FRANCIS-RUSSELL DESIGN-DECORATION, INC. wanted to create a light, comfortably inviting living room which could be used by an active family "summering" in the Hamptons. The room's natural light was minimal, available only from a single window and French doors. To compensate, the designers dropped the ceiling and installed high hat lighting which washed the creamy walls and overstuffed custom furnishings with a golden glow. The existing fireplace was tiled and faux painted, providing a cozy spot for afternoon tea. Bamboo chairs are from Hyde Park Antiques. PHOTOGRAPHY BY PETER VITALE PHOTOGRAPHY

RIGHT & OPPOSITE

"Any space, no matter how awkward or small, can be reinvented to satisfy the most sublime whimsy," said Michael Simon of MICHAEL SIMON INTERIORS, INC. of the tiny rectangular maid's room he transformed into a glowing jewel box. He designed this "Petit Salon" for the CRI • DESIGNER SHOW HOUSE in New York City, in the late 18th-century style using Nattier blue, putty, and mink wall panels, accented with gold-leaf moldings, faux stone columns, and painted limestone floors. With restrained opulence, Simon placed a 1780s' canapé from his personal collection into an alcove. By framing the niche in custom-woven taffeta, he highlighted the motifs of the 18th-century mantel. PHOTOGRAPHY BY TIM LEE

THIS PAGE

The living/media room by Samuel Botero of SAMUEL BOTERO ASSOCIATES, INC. created for the KIPS BAY BOYS & GIRLS CLUB DECORATOR SHOW HOUSE in New York City is an eclectic mélange of plush furniture, harmonious color and state-of-the-art electronic equipment. Botero designed the wall unit to house all media equipment and commissioned artist Stephen Spera to wrap the exterior with a serigraph incorporating newsprint headlines. Most of the furniture is designed by Botero for his retail collection including the pair of burgundy Ergorama chairs and the Arc sofa and console. While contemporary in feeling, the room is influenced by antiquity. A serene 10th-century Buddha and a 17th-century Japanese screen are expertly mixed with a Gothic Revival desk from Newell Galleries and antique bobbin-turned chair from Frederick P. Victoria & Son. PHOTOGRAPHY BY © PHILLIP ENNIS

The entrance of the manor house hosting the OAK & IVY SHOW HOUSE AND GARDEN in Montclair, New Jersey, was graced with beautifully aged English oak paneling. Designers Melinda and Michael Johnson of BOXWOOD HOUSE, INC. decided on a lived-in look for the space instead of the customary gallery setting. As counterpoint to the rich, dark wood, the design team selected comfortable, cream colored furniture for the fireplace seating area. The dark needlepoint rug is mindful of heavy traffic. Facing the front door is a pearwood console with graceful hurricane lamps, from John Rosselli. English Victorian bamboo antiques hold pictures and keepsakes. PHOTOGRAPHY BY © PHILLIP ENNIS

THIS PAGE & OPPOSITE BELOW

A small unattractive utility room was timelessly transformed into a study of seemingly larger scale at MANSIONS IN MAY in Morristown, New Jersey, by Marilee Schempp of DESIGN I. By using a dark matte pewter paint on the walls and steel colored stain on the pine floor, she emphasized the white architectural detail of the room. Jewel-toned silk taffeta pillows on a white daybed are introduced for visual impact.   PHOTOGRAPHY BY © PHILLIP ENNIS

OPPOSITE ABOVE

Ann Beard of ANN BEARD INTERIORS designed a patriotic library around an impressive collection of military artifacts and historical Americana from the 19th century for the JUNIOR LEAGUE OF NASHVILLE DECORATORS' SHOW HOUSE in Tennessee. The grandeur of the home at West Meade Farms was enhanced by her bold color statement and generous use of custom quilted fabric for the thirteen-foot-tall windows. An American flag from 1835 is framed above the carved mantle. The designer painted the walls a rich fatigue green as a backdrop to the red, white, and blue. A collection of 400 antique leather bound books lines the shelves.   PHOTOGRAPHY BY MICHAEL LEWIS PHOTOGRAPHY

A warm and inviting living room of the PHILHARMONIC HOUSE OF DESIGN in San Juan Capistrano, California, welcomes guests to sit on comfortable slipcovered furniture. The generous proportions of the room called for plentiful seating, so the designer, Randy Boyd, assisted by Nancy Fay of THURSTON/BOYD INTERIOR DESIGN, created two sitting areas—one facing the rich wood paneled wall and fireplace, and the other, in front of large windows. The designers combined period furnishings, mixing fabrics and patterns to give the room inviting appeal.

PHOTOGRAPHY BY SCOTT ROTHWALL PHOTOGRAPHY © 1997

Myriad textures and patterns combine in this loggia by Jennifer Garrigues, Allison Paladino, and Margaret Poetz of JENNIFER GARRIGUES, INC. for the AMERICAN RED CROSS DESIGNERS' SHOWHOUSE in West Palm Beach, Florida. Fringed and tasseled pillows are casually thrown on a plump paisley and Madagascar-cloth borne. The designer upholstered the antique wrought-iron campaign bed in chenille with jewel-toned fringe, hung curtains from bamboo poles, and illuminated the room with an Italian silk chandelier. PHOTOGRAPHY BY BARRY KINSELLA

A garden room designed with an eclectic mix of casual furnishings is enhanced by arched French doors that fill the space with a wash of sunlight. "The Orangerie," designed by Mario Villa of MARIO VILLA, INC. for the JUNIOR LEAGUE OF NEW ORLEANS DECORATORS' SHOW HOUSE VIII in Louisiana, is an irresistible spot for family relaxation and entertaining. The walls, painted in faux limestone with black marble border, resemble those of a centuries-old Tuscan villa. Wild flowers were painted onto the carpet that covers a granite floor. After sunset, a candlelit chandelier provides a warm glow. PHOTOGRAPHY BY DAVID RICHMOND/NEW ORLEANS

A once colorless space with small recessed windows in the BUCKS COUNTY DESIGNER HOUSE in Solebury, Pennsylvania, was given a Mission-style pedigree by Sally Dunn and Noreen Dunn, of HENDRIXSON'S FURNITURE. The designers chose to maintain the early-20th-century mood of the home by using pieces from their Stickley collection. A new terra-cotta tile floor is punctuated by a patterned Tibetan carpet. PHOTOGRAPHY BY RANDL BYE

A grand prewar apartment building set the stage for the ANSONIA CONDOMINIUM SHOWCASE in New York City. When designer Norman Michaeloff of NORMAN MICHAELOFF INTERIOR DESIGN, INC. first viewed his assigned rooms, he immediately decided to restore them to their original glory. Period moldings were added and the walls painted taupe. Michaeloff's living room was designed for a single mother whose daughter sleeps in the only bedroom. The living room has an elegant sofa which converts to a full-size bed. To save space, all media equipment is built-in.
PHOTOGRAPHY BY TIM LEE

Dramatic combinations of green define this ballroom-sized room of the HUDSON RIVER DESIGNER SHOWHOUSE in South Nyack, New York. Anthony Antine of ANTINE ASSOCIATES, INC. created two sitting areas to make a large space more intimate, covering the furniture in Brunschwig & Fils velvets and silks in varying shades of deep jade. The gilded tone of the Queen Anne style chinoiserie secretary, a piece from Antine's own line of furniture, resonates in the pale chartreuse on the walls. A girandole mirror sets off the gilded crown molding.   PHOTOGRAPHY BY TIM LEE

ABOVE LEFT & RIGHT

The Grand Salon designed by Bebe Winkler of BEBE WINKLER INTERIOR DESIGN, INC. for the CRI•DESIGNER SHOW HOUSE in New York City, is an amalgam of rich silk fabrics, elegant European furnishings, and fine art. Bold striped upholstered walls, which underscore ornate crown moldings, harmonize with the richly patterned wool carpet. PHOTOGRAPHY BY TIM LEE

Claudia Aquino of CLAUDIA AQUINO INTERIORS designed this family room for the DECORATORS' SHOW HOUSE in Atlanta, Georgia. Aquino incorporated the colors of Monet's home at Giverny, and painted the ceiling bright blue. "Sometimes when you apply a strong color. . . it brings the ceiling down a little and makes the room cozier," said the designer. She carefully mixed watercolor prints with neutral damask, and balanced them with the aged patina of French country antique furniture. PHOTOGRAPHY BY © DAVID SCHILLING

BELOW LEFT

At the MANSIONS & MILLIONAIRES DESIGNERS' SHOWCASE in Old Westbury, New York, a relaxed yet elegant library was given English country appeal by Megan de Roulet of WINDHAM HOUSE. She expertly blended sunny floral chintz with velvet stripes and wool plaids. The furnishings are an eclectic mix of European styles and sources. The ottoman is covered with a French Aubusson fragment, and two mahogany hall chairs with unusual painted medallions are English. PHOTOGRAPHY BY MARK SAMU PHOTOGRAPHY

BELOW RIGHT

This living room is defined by casual elegance at the JUNIOR LEAGUE OF NEW ORLEANS DECORATORS' SHOW HOUSE VIII in Louisiana. Designers Alix Rico and Patricia Brinson of DESIGN SOURCE gave the space a relaxed and intimate feel using light damask slipcovered furniture and voluminous silk drapes that puddle softly from a simple iron rod. To counter the scale of the two armchairs, the designers placed a bouillotte table. A large square ottoman with antiqued gold legs is covered in stenciled suede cloth and used as a coffee table. PHOTOGRAPHY BY DAVID RICHMOND/NEW ORLEANS

Jula Sutta and Dan Dunaway of SUTTADUNAWAY INC. chose a sophisticated palette of pale neutrals to create a welcoming sitting room at the SAN FRANCISCO UNIVERSITY HIGH SCHOOL DECORATOR SHOWCASE in California. Using furniture they designed for their own collection, the designers divided a long narrow space into two separate seating areas and anchored each with bookcases inspired by Japanese ikebana forms. Burnished ochre walls inspired by Italian palazzos provide a rich backdrop for the contemporary silk upholstered pieces with ebonized bases. PHOTOGRAPHY BY © KEN GUTMAKER ARCHITECTURAL PHOTOGRAPHY 1997

The transformation of a small 19th-century farmhouse into the BUCKS COUNTY DESIGNER HOUSE in Solebury, Pennsylvania, was no easy task. Designers Linda and Richard Delier, and James Gill of THE INTERIOR SHOP utilized the barn's largest space, the "great room," for their French country living/dining room. All French fabrics, cotton jacquards and rich velvets in warm shades of yellow, green and red, come from Pierre Frey. English antiques and accessories enabled the team to create a cozy European retreat deep in the heart of an American home. PHOTOGRAPHY BY RANDL BYE

Kathryn Ogawa and Gilles Depardon of OGAWA/ DEPARDON ARCHITECTS conceived their 350-square-foot living room at the ANSONIA CONDOMINIUM SHOWCASE in New York City, for an imaginary older couple with grown children. The furnishings, made of natural materials like wood, brushed steel, and sisal, were chosen for flexibility. Custom-designed ash tables can be used for intimate dinners or easily pushed together for large family gatherings. Overnight guests obtain privacy from a linen curtain surrounding the sofa.   PHOTOGRAPHY BY TIM LEE

In this living room at the SHOW HOUSE AT THE SHORE in Ventnor, New Jersey, John Kelly of JOHN KELLY INTERIOR DESIGN, INC. chose to open up the space using balanced asymmetry. Instead of placing the sofas and cocktail table in front of the fireplace, Kelly offset the furniture arrangement and gave equal importance to a striking Baldwin baby grand player piano. Oversized accessories complement the living room's grand scale.

PHOTOGRAPHY BY BARRY HALKIN

African mementos and photographs acquired on an imaginary safari served as inspiration for Kathryne A. Dahlman of KATHRYNE DESIGNS in this multipurpose family room. Designed for the PASADENA SHOWCASE HOUSE OF DESIGN in California, this 800-square-foot space was large enough to boast a number of seating areas for entertaining including a game room, bar, and of course, a state-of-the-art media area. Iron chandeliers shine on a faux leopard print carpet and Jerusalem stone flooring. Animal print pillows underscore the safari theme. PHOTOGRAPHY BY DAVID VALENZUELA PHOTOGRAPHY

A collection of primitive masks is showcased on paneled walls of a study at the PASADENA SHOWCASE HOUSE OF DESIGN in California. Marc Reusser and Debra Bergstrom of REUSSER BERGSTROM ASSOCIATES created a relaxed environment by combining multiple serendipitous elements with warm neutral colors. The ebonized Indonesian round table works surprisingly well with Biedermeier-style chairs. Natural color denim provides a casual slipcover for a tailored love seat.

PHOTOGRAPHY BY GREY CRAWFORD

BELOW

A Tudor vernacular, replete with original leaded windows and grandiose proportions, was the impetus for the grand gentleman's retreat by James Rixner of JAMES RIXNER INC. Set in the DECORATOR SHOWHOUSE in Oyster Bay, New York, the space takes on an air of polished refinement with Biedermeier furniture and a soft palette of camel and gray. A damask daybed, washed with sunlight, blends harmoniously with the decor.   PHOTOGRAPHY BY BILL ROTHSCHILD

A light-filled solarium in the DECORATORS' SHOW HOUSE in Atlanta, Georgia, became a perfect venue for reading and writing when Ann W. Platz of ANN PLATZ & COMPANY dressed it in sunny colors, botanical fabrics and traditional English-style furniture. The garden theme was carried out through the floral sofa and side chairs, and the custom-designed wool rug. A gilded secretary fits snugly into a small alcove. PHOTOGRAPHY BY PRO STUDIO, ATLANTA

NEXT SPREAD

In the ANSONIA CONDOMINIUM SHOWCASE set in an apartment building in New York City, characteristically small rooms were designed to fulfill real-life needs of typical Manhattanites. City living rooms often double as family rooms and libraries, so their furnishings have to be multifunctional and practical. Jorge Letelier and Sheryl Asklund Rock of LETELIER & ROCK DESIGN, INC. designed the pieces to conform to the circular shape of the space. Bleached ash-framed furniture, some with zip-off washable slipcovers, are framed to hold books. The wire and parchment sculpture is by Chilean artist, Palolo Valdez. PHOTOGRAPHY BY TIM LEE

Say au revoir and so long to the cold and lifeless rooms adjacent to the kitchen. Today, the dining room satisfies an assortment of tastes and pleasures. It is a salon for the epicurean, an intimate haven for dining à deux, or a cozy nook for a midnight snack. The dining room has become a multipurpose area within the house; often a study or library, where a period table and Chippendale chairs may have a use beyond dinner for six. In the showhouse dining room, among the most welcoming and personalized spaces created by designers, we are invited guests, enjoying the hospitality of the family who "lives" here.

DINING ROOMS

PREVIOUS SPREAD & RIGHT

Designers Carole Smith Harston and Marie Hayden of GABBERTS FURNITURE & DESIGN STUDIO created a refined yet cozy dining room for the TARRANT COUNTY HISTORIC PRESERVATION DESIGNER SHOWHOUSE in Euless, Texas. Mellow golden tones in the pine furnishings are brought to life when contrasted with vibrant reds and warm greens. A dining table by Baker highlights a collection of export porcelain displayed in the corner cupboard by Henredon.

PHOTOGRAPHY BY STEVE EDMONDS

BELOW & FAR RIGHT

An inviting oval shaped central hallway doubles as social hub and dining room for this chic cosmopolitan apartment at the ANSONIA CONDOMINIUM SHOWCASE in New York City. Designer Gail Green of GREEN & COMPANY, INC. INTERIOR DESIGNERS achieved a "mood moderne" by using forms and furnishings inspired by the Art Deco period. When not in use for dining, a circular Lalique glass table is easily moved aside into the rounded niche.

PHOTOGRAPHY BY © PHILLIP ENNIS & TIM LEE

Flooded with sunshine, this handsome dining area, designed by Marshall Watson of MARSHALL WATSON INTERIORS, LTD. is a component of an inviting living room which had once served as the public courtroom. Set in MANSIONS IN MAY in Morristown, New Jersey, the space recalls a luxurious gentlemen's club of the 1930s and 1940s, now updated to last into the next millennium. All the furniture was designed by Watson for Lewis Mittman, Inc. The library/dining table is set for a midnight snack. A high-backed banquette is imaginatively employed for seating. PHOTOGRAPHY BY © MICK HALES

The dining room designed by Jacqueline Epstein of JACQUELINE'S INTERIOR DESIGN STUDIO, INC. for the SHOWHOUSE AT THE SHORE in Ventnor, New Jersey, has a beautiful view of the ocean just outside its French doors. By faux painting the walls in a two-inch sand laden stripe with an antique glaze, Epstein made the room casually elegant and inviting. Gold leaf accentuates the moldings and the mirror above the fireplace. PHOTOGRAPHY BY ALEXANDER ANTON/STUDIO 53

Inspired by ancient European villas, Jeannie McKeogh of JEANNIE MCKEOGH INTERIORS decided to accentuate classic Italian romanticism with contemporary panache. In her dining room for the JUNIOR LEAGUE OF NEW ORLEANS DECORATORS' SHOW HOUSE VIII in Louisiana, she cleverly juxtaposed an antique Venetian table with a new brushed stainless old-world chandelier. The cane back chairs, custom painted and gilded by the designer, were made in Italy. McKeogh also painted the walls with designs derived from 17th- and 18th-century murals. PHOTOGRAPHY BY KERRI MCCAFFETY

In keeping with the style of this baronial Long Island manor home, Jennifer Garrigues of JENNIFER GARRIGUES, INC. staged an English country "hunt" breakfast at the DECORATOR SHOWHOUSE in Oyster Bay, New York. To create a rich European ambiance, she incorporated some of the home's original furnishings including a refectory table, a rich coral antique Persian rug, and a pair of 18th-century coromandel screens with English Chippendale-style mahogany ribbon back chairs.   PHOTOGRAPHY BY BILL ROTHSCHILD

Altogether exotic, this dining room for the DIVINE DESIGN SHOWHOUSE in Los Angeles, California, was the fanciful creation of Richard A. Cannon and Richard P. Bullock of CANNON/BULLOCK. Titled, "Pomegranates and Dates," it is a romantic retreat for two, enlivened with warm golden tones and punctuated with rich red and cobalt blue. The floor made of birdseed provides contrast to the gold leafed wall.   PHOTOGRAPHY BY ©CAMERON CAROTHERS PHOTOGRAPHY

The PHILHARMONIC HOUSE OF DESIGN in San Juan Capistrano, California set the stage for this traditional English country dining room. Michael Carey of MICHAEL CAREY INTERIOR DESIGN, INC. employed tea-stained floral fabric, plush velvet, gleaming wood and soft lighting for romantic appeal. The dining table and chairs are from Ralph Lauren and all chandeliers are French Art Deco. The hall adjacent to the dining room has similarly upholstered linen walls. PHOTOGRAPHY BY SCOTT ROTHWALL PHOTOGRAPHY © 1997

PREVIOUS SPREAD

The elegant dining room by Billy W. Francis and Ed Russell of FRANCIS-RUSSELL DESIGN-DECORATION, INC. was planned to blend effortlessly with the stately English Tudor home presenting the PASADENA SHOWCASE HOUSE OF DESIGN in California. A French chandelier gleams over a round table, which is draped with a Scalamandré silk cloth and seats fourteen comfortably. The breakfront is Biedermeier and the antique French carpet, selected to soften the room, dates from the 19th century.   PHOTOGRAPHY BY MARTIN FINE PHOTOGRAPHY

ABOVE

Peter Charles Lopipero of PETER CHARLES ASSOCIATES, LTD. used elements of country French style in a formal dining room of the LONG ISLAND HISTORIC ESTATES DESIGNER SHOW HOUSE in St. James, New York. The blush colors of an Aubusson rug are accented by Louis XV dining chairs, while an elegantly carved buffet and graceful vitrine display a collection of fine European porcelain and serving pieces.   PHOTOGRAPHY BY DON GORMLY

This ornate and architecturally distinguished room was once devoid of moldings and elegant details. Designer Barbara Ostrom of BARBARA OSTROM ASSOCIATES, INC. miraculously transformed an awkward space into a most impressive dining salon for the CRI • DESIGNER SHOW HOUSE in New York City. Columns, moldings and a coffered ceiling were added to the adjacent elevator foyer to balance an off-centered fireplace. Floors, which were in terrible condition, were painted to look like inlaid marquetry and all the walls were upholstered with rich damask from Gray Watkins. The English antique table and chairs are from Hyde Park Antiques.   PHOTOGRAPHY BY TIM LEE

OPPOSITE & LEFT

Inspired by the past, Michael Love of INTERIOR OPTIONS designed an intimate dining space for the OAK & IVY SHOW HOUSE AND GARDEN in Montclair, New Jersey, that speaks to today's modern sensibilities. Paying tribute to the grid patterns used by Charles Rennie Mackintosh, Love added signature squares to the wood paneling and repeated these shapes throughout the room. Unable to remove the existing fireplace surround, the designer refaced it with a new overmantel. Pale wood furniture is angled dramatically in front of the fireplace. PHOTOGRAPHY BY TIM LEE

BELOW LEFT & RIGHT

This informal dining area was created by Sig Bergamin of SIG BERGAMIN ARQUITETURA for CASA COR in São Paulo, Brazil. The composition of round table and banquette seating resembles a dining area on a luxurious yacht. Two bamboo chinoiserie chairs painted white echo the louvres of the solarium's shutters.

PHOTOGRAPHY BY TUCA REINÉS

OPPOSITE

This traditional dining room in the DECORATOR SHOWHOUSE in Oyster Bay, New York, exudes sophistication without pretense. Diane Knight, of K-II DESIGNS, LTD., used an animal print from Scalamandré on the windows, and repeated the motif in the art and accessories. A refined Federal-style sideboard flanked by black and gilded chairs offers a study in symmetry.　PHOTOGRAPHY BY BILL ROTHSCHILD

ABOVE

Light and airy, this inviting dining room in the CHARLESTON SYMPHONY ORCHESTRA LEAGUE DESIGNER SHOWHOUSE in South Carolina, was designed by Margaret Donaldson of MARGARET DONALDSON INTERIORS. A floral chinoiserie wallcovering from Scalamandré and a softly colored custom carpet establish the traditional tone.　PHOTOGRAPHY BY LESLIE WRIGHT DOW

LEFT & NEXT SPREAD

Designer Pam Kelker of CASTLES INTERIORS created this dining room for the DESIGNER SHOWHOUSE in Denver, Colorado. Kelker imbued the space with elegant, contemporary flare using brilliant color and bold furnishings. The walls, lacquered a rich red, are hand waxed with French polish. Bergère dining chairs, covered in playful Zebra stripes, are mixed with Queen Anne side chairs upholstered in an African inspired jungle print. Playing up this theme is a chandelier whimsically supported by a monkey with leopard lampshades.

PHOTOGRAPHY BY RON RUSCIO PHOTOGRAPHY

Today's kitchen is the most multifunctional, hardworking, and sociable room in our homes. As an anchor of family activities, it presents a vital space for designers to respond dynamically to lifestyle demands and kitchen functions. Equal attention is given to purpose and visual appeal in order for the kitchen to be a practical extension of the home's interior. The showhouse designer provides increasingly user-friendly kitchens with the latest technologically advanced appliances and ergonomically sound layouts. Craftsmanship and choice of materials are paramount, offering great ideas that are highly customized to fit a multitude of needs.

KITCHENS

PREVIOUS SPREAD & THIS PAGE

Johnny Grey and Joan Picone of JOHNNY GREY AND COMPANY created a bright space for the KIPS BAY BOYS & GIRLS CLUB DECORATOR SHOW HOUSE in New York City, that highlights the principles of their innovative kitchen design. As the hub of the home, it invites all family members to socialize, gather comfortably or participate in meal preparation. The unfitted nature of their kitchen "furniture," custom fabricated in Britain by Grey, boasts ergonomic shapes and work surfaces of varying heights. A reachable plate rack rests just above their signature raised dishwasher. PHOTOGRAPHY BY JASON SCHMIDT

OPPOSITE

The design of this compact kitchen by John A. Buscarello of JOHN A. BUSCARELLO, INC. in the ANSONIA CONDOMINIUM SHOWCASE in New York City, is sensitive to an empty nester whose mobility has been limited by arthritis. Rich cherry Wood-Mode cabinets have oversized pulls made of upside-down hooks. Above the breakfast counter, a special collection of easy grip ceramic dishes by Marusya is housed on open shelves. In the sink, a lever above the spout effortlessly controls the faucet. Blue retro bar stools by the Pace Collection echo the tone of the wall tiles and countertops. PHOTOGRAPHY BY TIM LEE

The elegant architecture of the JUNIOR LEAGUE OF GREATER PRINCETON SHOWHOUSE in New Jersey inspired this revitalization of a charming old-world kitchen by Francis C. Klein, Gottfried Bierbacher, and Maria Bucci of FRANCIS C. KLEIN AND ASSOCIATES, ARCHITECTS. Choosing a gray-blue & white color scheme, Barbara Pelly of BARBARA PELLY ASSOCIATES boldly accentuated the white custom cabinetry. Antique light fixtures from Urban Archaeology and simple brass hardware set the period tone. A new Thermador range and hood sit in front of the original white brick chimney. The smoky blue color of granite countertops extends to the patterns and stripes of the built-in breakfast nook.

PHOTOGRAPHY BY MELABEE M. MILLER

To retain the old-world look of the DECORATORS' SHOW HOUSE in Atlanta, Georgia, designer Jackie Naylor of JACKIE NAYLOR INTERIORS INC. and her associate, Kathleen Beres, were required to leave the original cabinets, sink, and marble countertops in place. Ripped vinyl flooring, peeling plaster, and antiquated appliances were replaced with dark green slate floor tiles, chamois colored faux fresco walls, and a new stove and refrigerator. New cabinets with modern storage alternatives blend with the old, and are unified by a shiny coat of green. PHOTOGRAPHY BY © ROBERT THIEN

RIGHT

Michael Love of INTERIOR OPTIONS designed a family kitchen in a modest-sized apartment of the ANSONIA CONDOMINIUM SHOWCASE in New York City. Using ready-made IKEA cabinets, she created a clean multifunctional space to be used by a young family for meal preparation, eating, playing and craftmaking. The stenciled countertop wraps around to become a dining and work surface on chrome legs. Tall ladder-back chrome chairs can be adjusted as needed to differing heights. PHOTOGRAPHY BY TIM LEE

ABOVE RIGHT & OPPOSITE

Michaela Scherrer of MICHAELA SCHERRER & ASSOCIATES designed a butler's pantry at the PASADENA SHOWCASE HOUSE OF DESIGN in California, to be efficient and user-friendly. The spare look of clean white cabinets, cool gray counters, and see-through doors and drawers is warmed by a comfortable cork floor laid in an Art Deco pattern. A light airy feeling is heightened by suspended glass shelves. PHOTOGRAPHY BY MICHAEL E. GARLAND

This kitchen was outfitted for the next millennium by Kimberley Fiterman of KFD Designs, Ltd. for the Ansonia Condominium Showcase in New York City. It was intended to be totally functional as well as visually exciting. To open up the space, the designer used a mirrored backsplash and brushed stainless steel cabinets. Countertops are blue pearl granite and the floors are set in a diamond pattern using granite and slate.   Photography by Tim Lee

This Page

For this bachelor's loft in Casa Cor in Curitiba, Brazil, designer Brunete Fraccaroli of Brunete Fraccaroli Arquitetura E Interiores planned a space where rooms seemlessly flow from one into another, divided only by furniture and glass walls. The loft's clean modernist sensibility is evident in the blue and white color scheme with countertops and floors of pure blond wood. · Photography by João Ribeiro

THIS SPREAD

In the DECORATOR SHOWHOUSE in Oyster Bay, New York, designers Sari Feuer and Stephen Kazantzis of EURO CONCEPTS, LTD. created a powerful kitchen that is ready for the next century. They chose Sokee cabinetry in warm beech and sleek stainless steel, replete with ample storage and modern conveniences for a family that likes to cook. A large center island is topped with a Franke sink and Carrara marble counter. A triangular butcher block table provides yet another handy place for cooking chores. PHOTOGRAPHY BY BILL ROTHSCHILD

ABOVE & RIGHT

The genteel mood of a bygone era, when the lady of the house planned the meals and staff members polished the silver, was the inspiration for a butler's pantry in the JUNIOR LEAGUE OF GREATER PRINCETON SHOWHOUSE in New Jersey. Designer Diane Carroll, of TRADITIONS, LTD. created a gracious atmosphere in keeping with the home's grand design. With minimal structural changes but maximum decorative detailing, the L-shaped area was transformed into an elegant multipurpose room—for laundry, china display, and wine storage. A "staging area" replete with gilded console, is used to serve formal dinners, as it is directly adjacent to the dining room and kitchen. Iron gates replaced doors to a small closet, which is now used as a wine storeroom.   PHOTOGRAPHY BY RALPH BOGERTMAN

FAR RIGHT

Relaxed and informal, this multipurpose kitchen/family room was created by Daniel Mullay of BLOOMINGDALE'S for MANSIONS IN MAY in Morristown, New Jersey. Rich honey toned mahogany floors and ceiling beams are offset by clean lined white cabinetry. Morning sunshine pours in through a large arched window draped with floral fabric from Lee Jofa. Bamboo and rattan chairs from Bloomingdale's complete the casual atmosphere.
PHOTOGRAPHY BY BILL ROTHSCHILD

THIS SPREAD

The kitchen by Jamie Drake of DRAKE DESIGN ASSOCIATES, INC. for the AMERICAN HOSPITAL OF PARIS FRENCH DESIGNER SHOWHOUSE in New York City, could be a lesson in stainless style. The narrow galley, illuminated by fluorescent "skylights," is highlighted by a commercial style stainless steel Thermador range and oversized Sub-Zero refrigerator. The icy blue terrazzo floor by Bisazza Italia is reflected in the cool tones of the appliances. Existing cabinets, left in situ, were polished a complementary blue. The sculptural Noguchi table and 1926 chairs by Mart Stam sparkle in the breakfast area. A cook's planning center is punctuated with blue laminate shelves. PHOTOGRAPHY BY © PETER PEIRCE

RIGHT

LeAnne Tamaribuchi of LEANNE TAMARIBUCHI INTERIOR DESIGN, with assistance from Cheryl Rader, transformed a butler's pantry into a warm and functional space in the PHILHARMONIC HOUSE OF DESIGN in San Juan Capistrano, California, by opening up the area with clever use of light, color, glass, and elegant antiques. Time-worn oak cabinets were rubbed with sage green paint to achieve an antique finish. Wood paneled cabinet doors were replaced with beveled glass. A Victorian brass faucet and granite countertop add to the old-world appeal.
PHOTOGRAPHY BY BERGER/CONSER PHOTOGRAPHY

BELOW

This breakfast room kitchen designed by Mark A. Polo of POLO M.A., INC. for the HUDSON RIVER DESIGNER SHOWHOUSE in South Nyack, New York, evokes old-world charm with modern convenience. Original wood cabinetry was given a dark glaze and new moldings. Coordinating checkerboard terra-cotta and white ceramic tiles of the countertop echo the floor and stenciled border.   PHOTOGRAPHY BY PETER PAIGE

OPPOSITE

This kitchen was designed by Sharon M. Reineke of SANDCASTLES, PROPERTY DESIGN & DEVELOPMENT, INC. for the CASTILLO DE ARENA DESIGNER SHOWHOUSE in Fort Lauderdale, Florida, with the serious cook in mind. All the English pine cabinetry was designed in cooperation with Dan Martinez of Haworth Country Furniture and custom built in England. To achieve an aged look, all components were distressed, stained with a golden color, and hand waxed. A new gas range by Viking punctuates the classicism of granite countertops.
PHOTOGRAPHY BY © IMAGE/DENNIS KRUKOWSKI

Sunshine floods an airy kitchen designed by Jamie Gibbs of JAMIE GIBBS AND ASSOCIATES for the CRI • DESIGNER SHOW HOUSE in New York City. Inspired by natural forms and the warm yellows and greens of a potager garden, this new French country kitchen transcends time. The branch-like counter edgings, leafy chandelier, and bronze drawer pulls adhere to the designer's "twig" motif. A marble baker's counter and breakfast bar compose a split-level center island, and to visually expand the space, the designer set terra-cotta floor tiles on the diagonal. Gibbs installed a U-Line wine cooler beneath the desk of the butler's hall, where a floral "rug" hand painted by Michael Walker echoes the wallpaper pattern.

PHOTOGRAPHY BY TIM EBERT PHOTOGRAPHY

BELOW LEFT

Beautiful wood sets a luxurious tone for this well equipped wine cellar in the PASADENA SHOWCASE HOUSE OF DESIGN in California. Peggy Hammerschmidt of HAMMER & SCHMIDT DESIGN harkened to medieval times when she turned an L-shaped space into a contemporary home for 400 bottles. Wall sconces, reminiscent of ancient torches, illuminate plaster walls which were hand burnished using a technique that dates to the Renaissance. Custom cabinetry is defined by vertical blocks of cherry and ebony, and a marble table forms a convenient surface for un-corking favorite wines.   PHOTOGRAPHY BY DAVID GLOMB

BELOW RIGHT

Bacchus holds court in a wine cellar created for the AMERICAN HOSPITAL OF PARIS FRENCH DESIGNER SHOWHOUSE in New York City, by Christine Hawley of CHRISTINE HAWLEY CUSTOM WINE CELLAR DESIGNS WITH SHERRY-LEHMANN, INC. "Bijou Cave" was inspired by the cellars of the great chateaux of Bordeau. With capacity for over 1000 bottles, the cellar is equipped with a gravel floor to maintain appropriate humidity levels and a vaulted ceiling illuminated by a candlelit fixture.

PHOTOGRAPHY BY ROBERT RIGGS

THIS PAGE

The breakfast nook of the PHILHARMONIC HOUSE OF DESIGN in California boasts a stunning view of the San Juan Capistrano Mission and the Pacific Ocean beyond. Designers Kay Leruth of LERUTH INTERIOR DESIGN and Kara Piller of PILLER DESIGN hung a copper chandelier from the hand painted ceiling to crown a circular wooden table. Comfortable high-backed chairs, tailored in quilted slipcovers, complement the dramatic bow window. Leruth and Piller collaborated on the spacious kitchen and balanced old-world charm with modern practicality. Opting to open up and update the space without removing the existing cabinets, the designers replaced oak paneled facades with black glass and stainless steel, and removed a massive overhead exhaust hood. All countertops were changed to sparkling granite and the center island was lightened with a biscuit cream base and tan overglaze.

PHOTOGRAPHY BY A.G. PHOTOGRAPHY

For the KIPS BAY BOYS & GIRLS CLUB DECORATOR SHOW HOUSE in New York City, Gail Green of GREEN & COMPANY, INC. INTERIOR DESIGNERS presented her idea of a cook's dream kitchen. Luminous stainless steel cabinets and appliances, offset by a polished marble floor, create a vintage look. Backsplash tiles in warm earth tones blend with ivory limestone countertops. A restaurant-type hooded range balances the seating area at the opposite end of the room.

PHOTOGRAPHY BY © PHILLIP ENNIS

RIGHT

Rochelle Kalisch of REGENCY KITCHENS INC. magically transformed a small and cramped kitchen into an elegantly functional area at the ANSONIA CONDOMINIUM SHOWCASE in New York City. Removing a wall between the kitchen and living room, the designer was able to create additional counter space and storage. She installed rich blond wood cabinets and enveloped the ceiling with the same veneer.

PHOTOGRAPHY BY TIM LEE

At the KIPS BAY BOYS & GIRLS CLUB DECORATOR SHOW HOUSE in New York City, Beverly Ellsley of BEVERLY ELLSLEY DESIGN created a sumptuous kitchen that looks like it dates to the original home. All appliances, with the exception of the stove, were hidden behind furniture-styled cabinetry. Using a gothic motif, the designer peaked the arches of the window valences to reinforce the lines of the upper cabinet doors. A marble "rug" set into the limestone floor beneath a center island looks like a well-worn antique. PHOTOGRAPHY BY © PHILLIP ENNIS

A draped bed of tailored ivory twill is the centerpiece of the master bedroom by Shelby de Quesada of SHELBY DE QUESADA INTERIOR DESIGN and Jorge de Quesada of DE QUESADA ARCHITECTS, INC. Layers of golden off-whites provide uniformity of tone that illuminates this space in the SAN FRANCISCO UNIVERSITY HIGH SCHOOL DECORATORS' SHOWCASE in California. An antique Tabriz rug underscores a collection of fine period pieces—an 18th-century secretary, Swedish neoclassic console, and a pair of Italian gilded armchairs upholstered in Fortuny damask.
PHOTOGRAPHY BY © KEN GUTMAKER ARCHITECTURAL PHOTOGRAPHY 1997

RIGHT & BELOW LEFT

This serene silvery blue and taupe bedroom was designed by Freya Surabian of FREYA SURABIAN DESIGN ASSOCIATES for the JUNIOR LEAGUE OF BOSTON DECORATORS' SHOWHOUSE in Massachusetts. Primarily a guest room, it is also a retreat for a visiting college-age daughter. This space is all about sophisticated, luxurious comfort. The bed and chairs are custom upholstered with fabrics from Brunschwig & Fils. Over a painted dresser hangs an impressive Venetian mirror.   PHOTOGRAPHY BY © SAM GRAY

BELOW RIGHT & OPPOSITE

A Scandinavian theme was selected by designers Lee Bierly and Christopher Drake of BIERLY-DRAKE ASSOCIATES, INC. for the symmetrical bedroom they designed for the JUNIOR LEAGUE OF BOSTON DECORATORS' SHOWHOUSE in Massachusetts. Fabrics and painted woods in soft whites, pale yellow and cream are offset by a vibrant green wall. The exquisite simplicity of the space is enriched by a subtle choice of Gustavian antiques and understated fine linens.
PHOTOGRAPHY BY © SAM GRAY

Dramatic color and luxurious fabrics make this man's bedroom in the HUDSON RIVER DESIGNER SHOWHOUSE in South Nyack, New York, a treat for the senses. Ho Sang Shin of ANTINE ASSOCIATES, INC. gave depth to a small room by layering tones of rust, clay, and cinnabar. An exotic tented daybed draped in velvet and silk from Manuel Canovas is fringed with black accents. PHOTOGRAPHY BY TIM LEE

THIS PAGE

A flowery golden wallpaper from Osborne & Little was chosen by designers Phyllis K. Avant and Tisha Borders of PHYLLIS AVANT INTERIORS, INC. to brighten a relatively dark master bedroom at the JUNIOR LEAGUE OF NASHVILLE DECORATORS' SHOW HOUSE in Tennessee. The carved French bed is crowned by an elegant canopy that coordinates with a draped dressing table. The overall look is one of genteel European elegance.

PHOTOGRAPHY BY BILL LAFEVOR

RIGHT

Old-world elegance and modern simplicity are the hallmarks of this romantic bedroom in the DECORATOR SHOWHOUSE in Oyster Bay, New York. Greg Lanza of GREG LANZA INTERIOR DESIGN placed the inviting silk upholstered bed in front of a deep bay window, making it seem to float outdoors. Lanza suspended unlined striped silk taffeta panels at the windows from ebony poles, echoing the leaded grid.

PHOTOGRAPHY BY TIM EBERT PHOTOGRAPHY

BELOW LEFT

Sheer netting mysteriously shrouds a bed and puddles beside an awning striped butterfly chair, setting an exotic tone for Ho Sang Shin's beachy bedroom in the SPRING LAKE SHOWHOUSE in New Jersey. The bed, created by the designer for ANTINE ASSOCIATES, INC. is covered with a bold Donghia print. Antique bamboo furniture adds a golden glow to the room. PHOTOGRAPHY BY TIM LEE

BELOW RIGHT & OPPOSITE

The MANSIONS & MILLIONAIRES DESIGNERS' SHOWCASE is an eclectic style 1920s' mansion in North Hills, New York. The triangular niches and alcoves in the penthouse master bedroom suite presented a design challenge for the team of ANNE ZUCKERBERG ASSOCIATES. To achieve an uninterrupted space, Anne Zuckerberg and her associate, Elise Kodish, flushed out one entire wall and provided the finished room with an eclectic display of design elements reminiscent of Paris salons. Zuckerberg placed a neoclassic settee accented with gold leaf and reproductions of Coco Chanel's bergères amidst a comfortable retreat of soothing neutrals.

PHOTOGRAPHY BY GEORGE ROSS

This master bedroom suite was designed by Michael deSantis of MICHAEL DeSANTIS, INC. to evoke images of grand summer retreats from Gatsby-era Long Island at the ROGERS MEMORIAL LIBRARY DESIGNERS' SHOWHOUSE in Southampton, New York. In order to unify the grand master bedroom suite and hide some of the interruptive windows and doors, he camouflaged the walls in folds of French vanilla linen and hung them from a border of wooden rosettes. The bed, made up in Anichini linens, is flanked by a pair of antique Dutch inlaid chests.

PHOTOGRAPHY BY © PHILLIP ENNIS

ABOVE LEFT & RIGHT

Myles Scott Harlan of MYLES SCOTT HARLAN INTERIOR DESIGN created a modern classic for this man's guestroom/study and outfitted it in cool haberdashery colors. He turned a tiny rear bedroom of the HUDSON RIVER DESIGNER SHOWHOUSE in South Nyack, New York, into a multifunctional mix of contemporary furnishings, 1950s' and 1960s' pieces, and a vintage white wool shag rug. A large silver leafed mirror leans against the wall behind the gray tweed daybed, visually increasing the size of the room. A glass topped desk with a pair of black and stainless steel pedestal bases was custom-made for the designer by The Pace Collection. Tailored tweed panels form neat window valences, and lime green accessories further define the charcoal and off-white forms.

PHOTOGRAPHY BY PETER MARGONELLI

LEFT

Designers Bruce Long and Robert Giberson of BRUCE NORMAN LONG imagined the room they created for the VASSAR SHOWHOUSE in Radnor, Pennsylvania as a quintessential gentleman's study/bedroom. Their first step was to paint the walls deep brown to promote depth and the ceiling sky blue to increase the appearance of height. Asymmetrical window treatments, made of unlined natural duck cloth, are elegant and maximize natural light. A handsome wood library table is used as a desk.

PHOTOGRAPHY BY © LEWIS TANNER

Susan Orsini of ORSINI DESIGN ASSOCIATES designed her small space for the KIPS BAY BOYS & GIRLS CLUB DECORATOR SHOW HOUSE in New York City, as a refined dressing room for a stylish, worldly woman. Her eclectic choice of antiques ranges from a Madagascar wood Art Deco dressing table to an Empire inspired bar cabinet, outfitted for shoes. An antique Japanese screen and French sconces contribute to the glamorous setting.   PHOTOGRAPHY BY © PETER PEIRCE

A turned wood mahogany fourposter bed holds court in this large and inviting master bedroom in the ST. LYONN DECORATOR SHOWHOUSE in Marietta, Georgia. Designer Cheryl Womack of CHERYL WOMACK INTERIORS mixed overstuffed upholstery with hand painted wood furniture and antiques to create a gracious room with ageless allure. PHOTOGRAPHY BY © ROBERT THIEN

Sensuous serenity best describes this room created for the AMERICAN RED CROSS DESIGNERS' SHOWHOUSE in West Palm Beach, Florida, by Lee Bierly and Christopher Drake of BIERLY-DRAKE ASSOCIATES, INC. Soft Scandinavian colors are found in the painted coffee-and-cream colored checkerboard floor and pearl gray walls. The romantic bed is draped in cool tailored linen fabric, contrasting with voluminous rose tinted taffeta drapes. The designers added generous crown molding and hung all drapery directly from the ceiling to create the illusion of greater height.
PHOTOGRAPHY BY © IMAGE/DENNIS KRUKOWSKI

BELOW LEFT & RIGHT

Susan Aiello of INTERIOR DESIGN SOLUTIONS, INC. brought a spring garden indoors to a pristine guest bedroom of the MANSIONS & MILLIONAIRES DESIGNERS' SHOWCASE in Old Westbury, New York. The centerpiece of the room—a collection of botanical watercolors by artist Cristine Piane—set the tone for window treatments of ivy and flowers, and a delicate wash of color on the walls. As a counterpoint to the room's softness of color and form, the designer selected furniture with simple, austere lines: a Louis Philippe daybed and a Regency plant stand.   PHOTOGRAPHY BY P. WHICHELOE

Designer Jacqueline Ann Cappa and John Cappa Jr. of LOCUST VALLEY DESIGN CENTER were given a large, beautifully square guest bedroom with a marble fireplace and traditional moldings to work with at the MANSIONS & MILLIONAIRES DESIGNERS' SHOWCASE in Lattingtown, New York. Creating a cocoon of luxury, they embellished the room with patterned upholstered walls and an Aubusson carpet. Attention to details, exemplified by the comforter which is trimmed on one side with buttons and the other with rosettes, contribute to the bedroom's sensuous appeal. PHOTOGRAPHY BY OLEG MARCH PHOTOGRAPHY

For the MANSIONS & MILLIONAIRES DESIGNERS' SHOWCASE in Old Westbury, New York, designers Richard L. Schlesinger and Lynn Gerhard of RICHARD L. SCHLESINGER INTERIORS produced an elegantly appointed guest bedroom where the occupants may be inclined to overstay their welcome. To visually expand the small space, the designers installed a diagonally patterned carpet and drapery panels over mirrored walls. An antique sunburst mirror, circa 1850, is one of many eye-catching decorative accessories.

PHOTOGRAPHY BY MARK SAMU PHOTOGRAPHY

Designers Stewart Silverman and Michael Cesario of STEWART MICHAEL DESIGN, INC. used vibrant red as the focal point of a golden taupe bedroom in the MANSIONS & MILLIONAIRES DESIGNERS' SHOWCASE in North Hills, New York. Walls were softened with a camel color and the room was anchored with ebony stained baseboard moldings. Taupe linen sheets by Anichini with gold scrolled border grace a French country bed that is covered in rouge matelassé. In the adjacent sitting room, rich claret walls make a strong impact. An early 20th-century French advertising poster is juxtaposed with a crescent love seat covered in golden damask.

PHOTOGRAPHY BY OLEG MARCH PHOTOGRAPHY

OPPOSITE & LEFT

The American West inspired Zeila Fachada of ZEILA FACHADA PLANEJAMENTO DE INTERIORES to create a rustic bedroom for CASA COR in São Paulo, Brazil. The designer created a cabin-like interior by applying exposed timbers to unadorned walls. An iron bed, layered with cozy quilts and plaid blankets, further enhances the western spirit.

PHOTOGRAPHY BY JOÃO RIBEIRO

BELOW

An eclectic bedroom designed for a student of architecture plays on a theme of geometric shapes and forms. Using myriad architectural references, Richard A. Cannon and Richard P. Bullock of CANNON/BULLOCK created the space for the PASADENA SHOWCASE HOUSE OF DESIGN in California. Chairs by the Pace Collection, covered in square sections of Camino Crispo wood, were influenced by the same period. Indonesian rice paddy lanterns flank the Art Deco style armoire.

PHOTOGRAPHY BY © CAMERON CAROTHERS PHOTOGRAPHY

The limited space of a fourteen-by-fourteen-foot guest bedroom in the CHARLESTON SYMPHONY ORCHESTRA LEAGUE DESIGNER SHOWHOUSE in South Carolina, was further restricted by six doors and two mismatched windows. To soften the irregular edges of the room, Karen Padgett Prewitt of QUATTRO CANTI INTERIORS bridged two closets with an arched soffit. In the newly created niche, the designer enlisted artist Karl Beckwith Smith to hand paint a flea market tin and iron bed with a rendering of the Florentine *Villa La Pietra*. To complete the serene Italianate mood and visually enlarge the space, Prewitt kept walls, moldings and fabrics neutral, and accented them with a judicious mix of antiques, affordable reproductions, mail-order catalog art, and a merino wool throw by Anichini linens.   PHOTOGRAPHY BY LESLIE WRIGHT DOW

OPPOSITE

The DESIGNER SHOW HOUSE in Woodbury, Connecticut, was staged in the 18th-century Van Vleck farmhouse. Although the master bedroom was in a severe state of disrepair, designer Cynthia Kasper of INTERIOR ACCENTS discovered its architectural bones—wide floorboards, and fine details. Walls were re-plastered and stenciled in a pattern created by the designer. Pristine English pelmets grace the room's small windows allowing sunshine to wash the space in light and a graceful Biedermeier chair creates a charming vignette in the room's steep eave.   PHOTOGRAPHY BY TIM LEE

RIGHT

Designer Anna Shay of SOLANNA fashioned an exotic safari inspired guestroom/den from a tiny attic space for the PHILHARMONIC HOUSE OF DESIGN in San Juan Capistrano, California. A steeply angled ceiling was upholstered in inexpensive canvas and jute rope to look like a tent with walls made of handmade block patterned paper from Nepal. A custom rosewood daybed of Anglo-Indian design is finished by hand with rubbed wax. PHOTOGRAPHY BY DAVID VALENZUELA PHOTOGRAPHY

BELOW

Pia Ledy of PIADESIGN INC. created a study in stripes for a teen bedroom in an apartment of the ANSONIA CONDOMINIUM SHOWCASE in New York City. To counter the linear patterns of the Mission-style bed, wallpaper, and linens, she chose fabrics with a touch of whimsy and a jazz-patterned rug. PHOTOGRAPHY BY TIM LEE

OPPOSITE

A silk taffeta balloon curtain, in a plaid of yellow, pink, and green, sets the color scheme for this romantic bedroom designed by Barbara Ostrom of BARBARA OSTROM ASSOCIATES, INC. for the ANSONIA CONDOMINIUM SHOWCASE in New York City. Comfortable soft furnishings are enveloped in luxurious fabrics and color, offset by richly appointed accessories. PHOTOGRAPHY BY TIM LEE

BELOW

One ap

KIPS

souven

CUNNIN

PREVIOUS SPREAD & ABOVE LEFT

An image of opulence and luxury is evoked in this bath and dressing room in the DECORATOR SHOWHOUSE in Oyster Bay, New York, by Richard Mishaan of RICHARD MISHAAN DESIGN. Previously an office next to the master bedroom, this new translation offers the gentleman of the house a place for contemplative thoughts and pampered relaxation. The designer combined ruggedly handsome furnishings with colors and fabrics that are light and airy. A spacious linen colored armoire houses the gentleman's suits and complements the linen and Nubuck chaise from the designer's own line of furniture.   PHOTOGRAPHY BY © PETER PEIRCE

RIGHT

Anne Zuckerberg and Elise Kodish of ANNE ZUCKERBERG ASSOCIATES created a Romanesque bathroom for the MANSIONS & MILLIONAIRES DESIGNERS' SHOWCASE in North Hills, New York, out of a quirky garret space. She paved the floor with Italian terra-cotta tiles inset with a large medallion of unpolished slate and marble. A French Empire chair, set against a cool backdrop of faux painted limestone walls, strikes a regal note.   PHOTOGRAPHY BY GEORGE ROSS

ABOVE RIGHT & OPPOSITE

The Gothic Revival manor staging the DECORATORS' SHOW HOUSE in Atlanta, Georgia, possessed wonderful mullioned windows. Designers Jackie Naylor and her associate, Kathleen Beres of JACKIE NAYLOR INTERIORS INC. incorporated them into their handsome bathroom scheme. Geometric shapes and angles are used in the diamond patterned limestone floor and the raised, sculptural sink set on the diagonal.   PHOTOGRAPHY BY © ROBERT THIEN

Designer Shelby de Quesada of SHELBY DE QUESADA INTERIOR DESIGN and architect Jorge de Quesada of DE QUESADA ARCHITECTS, INC. collaborated on these his-and-her bathroom suites. Created for the SAN FRANCISCO UNIVERSITY HIGH SCHOOL DECORATORS' SHOWCASE in California, the suites' understated elegance is underscored with details inspired by 1930s' Paris. The designers covered the walls and floors in a golden marble, which surrounds the nickel bordered medicine chest, shower and water closet enclosure. The fluid lines of the transom are polished nickel, while paneled walls in his bath are composed of African Makare mahogany. The focal point of her bath is a tub with marble surround and a breathtaking view of the bay from an arched window.   PHOTOGRAPHY BY © KEN GUTMAKER ARCHITECTURAL PHOTOGRAPHY 1997

A meager five-by-six-foot ground floor powder room of the KIPS BAY BOYS & GIRLS CLUB DECORATOR SHOW HOUSE in New York City was given a lush makeover by Ronald F. Wagner and Timothy Van Dam of WAGNER VAN DAM DESIGN & DECORATION. Using trompe l'oeil wallpaper by F. Schumacher & Co., they created the illusion of architectural detail, adding dimension to the space. The designer transformed the powder room into a fantasy garden by covering the floor in a limestone mosaic, enclosing the radiator in a wood trellis, and creating a sink from a 19th-century garden urn. The gold plated Sherle Wagner sink fittings are mounted fountain-style to a grand marble wall plaque.

PHOTOGRAPHY BY © PETER PEIRCE

This bathroom, enveloped in rich mahogany, was designed by James Rixner of JAMES RIXNER INC. for the KIPS BAY BOYS & GIRLS CLUB DECORATOR SHOW HOUSE in New York City. Contemporary nickel sconces illuminate the wood cabinetry and silver leaf tea paper ceiling.

PHOTOGRAPHY BY TOM MCCAVERA

Designer Michael M. Mariotti of MICHAEL MARIOTTI INTERIOR DESIGN took his color cue from existing pale green tiles when he transformed a bathroom and closet into a gentleman's dressing suite for the HUDSON RIVER DESIGNER SHOWHOUSE in South Nyack, New York. His use of Gothic Revival details, including the tile crown molding and a large mirror, relates to the architecture of the house.

PHOTOGRAPHY BY TIM EBERT PHOTOGRAPHY

LEFT

Jacqueline Ann Cappa and John Cappa Jr. of LOCUST VALLEY DESIGN CENTER created this inviting bathroom for the MANSIONS & MILLIONAIRES DESIGNERS' SHOWCASE in Old Westbury, New York. The walls were upholstered in the same luxurious fabric as the accompanying bedroom.   PHOTOGRAPHY BY OLEG MARCH PHOTOGRAPHY

BELOW LEFT

Designers Jackie Naylor and Kathleen Beres of JACKIE NAYLOR INTERIORS INC. were inspired by the botanical print wall covering they found in the existing powder room assigned to them for the DECORATORS' SHOW HOUSE in Atlanta, Georgia. Tearing away wallpaper right down to the sheetrock, they randomly painted faux stones which were washed with a milky translucent glaze to achieve a rich aged patina. The outdoor theme was continued by fashioning a sink from an amber glass bowl set on chiseled onyx.   PHOTOGRAPHY BY © ROBERT THIEN

RIGHT

Utilizing dark amber CyTron—a new synthetic material from Sirmos—Jamie Drake of DRAKE DESIGN ASSOCIATES, INC. wrapped the tub surround and gold glass sink for the ANSONIA CONDOMINIUM SHOWCASE in New York City, creating a look much like fine cabinetry. Amber tiles in the shower are offset by green and gold glass mosaic tiles from Bisazza.   PHOTOGRAPHY BY TIM LEE

A grand Mediterranean estate in Fort Lauderdale, Florida presented the CASTILLO DE ARENA DESIGNER SHOWHOUSE. Designer Sharon M. Reineke of SANDCASTLES, PROPERTY DESIGN & DEVELOPMENT, INC. wanted to draw upon the warm colors and rich elegant furnishings of centuries-old Italian villas for the master bathroom. Romanticism is her recurring theme, evident in the delicately embroidered valances, silver accessories and personal photographs. A large spa tub and matching sink are enveloped in custom-made Spanish cedar cabinetry. PHOTOGRAPHY BY © IMAGE/DENNIS KRUKOWSKI

A nautical inspired bath was designed by Cynthia F. Bennett of CYNTHIA BENNETT & ASSOCIATES, INC. for the PASADENA SHOWCASE HOUSE OF DESIGN in California. For the bathroom floor, the designers placed creamy travertine marble next to iridescent blue Raku tile to resemble a sandy beach, and the teak bench and shelving are held together with sailing rope. The glass shower features a custom molded ocean wave pattern and an aquarium mounted into the wall. PHOTOGRAPHY BY RACHEL OLGUIN

Trompe l'oeil and an English garden theme define an enchanted powder room for the PHILHARMONIC HOUSE OF DESIGN in San Juan Capistrano, California. Larry Froemmling of LAWRENCE DESIGN opened up a small windowless bathroom and transformed it into a romantic trellised gazebo. The toilet, cleverly hidden inside a wicker chaise, sits beneath a painted orange tree that decoratively grows up the wall and ceiling. In the lounge, a round marquetry mirror provides the illusion of added space. PHOTOGRAPHY BY A.G. PHOTOGRAPHY

A whimsical, brightly colored master bath was designed by William Spink of SPINK, INC. for the ANSONIA CONDOMINIUM SHOWCASE in New York City, as a private retreat for parents of young children. The wall covering is made of recycled newspaper, tissue paper and gold leaf. The large arched window is left unadorned to focus on the spectacular view, while a coffee maker, television and CD player provide ultimate convenience. PHOTOGRAPHY BY TIM LEE

Gwynneth R. Davis of RENWICK DESIGN spruced up a plain white bathroom at the JUNIOR LEAGUE OF GREATER PRINCETON SHOWHOUSE in New Jersey, by adding bright accents of bold color. A multicolored patchwork of fabric appears as a valence for the pedestal sink. Brass fixtures and lamps retain the period look.

Designers Raymond J. Cuminale and Scott Lalley of R. SCOTT LALLEY INTERIOR DESIGN transformed a banal bathroom into "L'Art de la Salle de Bain, à la Mondrian" for the AMERICAN HOSPITAL OF PARIS FRENCH DESIGNER SHOWHOUSE in New York City. Using Corian by DuPont as the medium, they wrapped the entire room with panels of red, blue and yellow, set against a stark white background. Making use of Mondrian's black grid pattern, they re-created his early-20th-century masterpiece.

ABOVE LEFT & RIGHT

Drama emanates from wispy tea-stained mosquito netting draped gracefully over a newly re-glazed white tub. Jackie Naylor and her associate, Kathleen Beres of JACKIE NAYLOR INTERIORS INC. performed a much needed facelift for an upstairs bathroom in the DECORATORS' SHOW HOUSE in Atlanta, Georgia. Removal of a tattered carpet revealed a vintage beige and white tile floor which served as a foil for whimsical accessories—a wood bath mat, plunger toilet tissue stand, and an old piano stool. PHOTOGRAPHY BY © ROBERT THIEN

LEFT & NEXT SPREAD

Gail Green of GREEN & COMPANY, INC. INTERIOR DESIGNERS combined design elements that are simultaneously traditional and modern in her master bathroom for the JUNIOR LEAGUE OF GREENWICH DESIGNER SHOWHOUSE in Connecticut. Using a style she refers to as "Regency Modern," green and white were paired to create a graceful airy space. One fabric, used throughout for visual harmony, was trimmed with playful oversized gold tassels. A pair of star-shaped sconces flank the French ribbon patterned gilded mirror. PHOTOGRAPHY BY © GAIL GREEN

Showhouse designers are often challenged with odd shaped spaces. This was the case when Katherine McCallum and Priscilla Ulmann of McMillen, Inc. tackled a pair of maids' rooms on the fifth floor of a mansion, and converted them into a lady's bower. The 22-foot-by-8-foot space in the Kips Bay Boys & Girls Club Decorator Show House in New York City possessed steep eaves, ceiling, and a set of barrel vaulted dormer windows. To achieve the ambiance of a garden shelter of woven branches, they covered the sloping walls and narrow ceiling with Chuck Fischer's twig wallpaper. The tumbled travertine floor is set in a herringbone pattern resembling a garden path, and the 19th-century Swedish secretary is made of birch wood.

PHOTOGRAPHY BY BILL ROTHSCHILD

ABOVE RIGHT

For the Rogers Memorial Library Designers' Showhouse in Southampton, New York, designer Albert E. Pensis of Pensis-Stolz Inc. kept the seaside location in mind when planning his retreat at the top of the stairs. A hand painted diamond patterned wall by Brian Garbe echoes the color of the ocean, and a majestic cherry secretary serves as display cabinet and writing table.

PHOTOGRAPHY BY BILL ROTHSCHILD

RIGHT

The Ansonia Condominium Showcase in New York City was the setting for this youthful celadon colored bachelor's living room by Maureen Crilly of Crilly Companies. Her palette was dictated by the metallic lacquered bar cabinet from Dakota Jackson, while a black leather chaise and brushed steel table were selected for easy care and high style. PHOTOGRAPHY BY TIM LEE

CASA COR in São Paulo, Brazil, had a small open terrace which Rosa May Sampaio of ROSA MAY SAMPAIO INTERIOR DESIGNER transformed using large glass windows to create a year-round winter garden. Complete with cozy fireplace, the room's naturalist theme is emphasized with fabrics such as sisal, jute, cotton and silk.
PHOTOGRAPHY BY ALAIN BRUGIER

Eugene Perreault of ENTASIS produced a masculine art collector's study for the library in the DECORATORS' SHOW HOUSE in Buckeystown, Maryland, replete with European sculpture, Italian engravings and an impressive mahogany desk with custom silver leaf ormolu. The walls, which were faux painted to look like 18th-century silver tea paper, set the color scheme and an ornamental zinc coated architectural facade hangs over the mantle.   PHOTOGRAPHY BY CHARLES MCMILLION

Designers Miriam Wohlberg and Pam Levy of WOHLBERG/LEVY DESIGNS, LTD. rendered their study for the CRI • DESIGNER SHOW HOUSE in New York City as a writer's atelier, inscribing the frieze around the room with words from different languages. The built-in cabinetry showcases a collection of typewriters and pens, and for the workaholic, the design team installed a coffee/bar/refrigerator unit.
PHOTOGRAPHY BY TIM LEE

OPPOSITE

When designer Marjorie Stark of MARJORIE STARK INTERIOR DESIGN first saw the attic she was assigned for the DESIGNER SHOWHOUSE in Denver, Colorado, she was challenged yet undaunted. Despite a 22-inch-wide door and virtually no ceiling, Stark created an ideal hideaway for a serious astronomy buff with clever use of drywall and faux painting.

PHOTOGRAPHY BY RON RUSCIO PHOTOGRAPHY

THIS PAGE

Brunete Fraccaroli of BRUNETE FRACCAROLI ARQUITETURA E INTERIORES named this room in CASA COR in São Paulo, Brazil, the "Collector's Room." Designed to be more than just a study, the space provides the owner of the house with a private area in which to appreciate and store a valuable collection of postage stamps. Fraccaroli mixed modern technology with an appreciation for the past by furnishing the room with new audiovisual equipment and custom-built wood cabinets equipped with drawers for organizing the stamps.   PHOTOGRAPHY BY JOÃO RIBEIRO

In order to create a whimsical adult retreat within the DECORATORS' SHOW HOUSE in Atlanta, Georgia, designer Murray Vise of J. MURRAY VISE INTERIOR DESIGN eschewed his typically conservative style for one of pure drama. The split-level space, formerly maid's quarters, was brought to life with vibrant color and fanciful furnishings. The Gothic inspired bookcase and writing desk echo the style of the manor house itself, while strong visual punch is achieved with a five cornered star mirror reflecting the room's odd shapes and angles. PHOTOGRAPHY BY © DAVID SCHILLING

Barbara Hauben-Ross of BARBARA HAUBEN-ROSS, INC. describes the library she designed with Lauder Bowden as "both real and virtual." At the KIPS BAY BOYS & GIRLS CLUB DECORATOR SHOW HOUSE in New York City, the designers transformed a nondescript dark wood paneled library into a comfortably elegant space using updated Art Deco classics and multimedia technology. Beginning with the room's structural bones, Hauben-Ross and Bowden converted the walls into a two-toned upholstered surface and crowned them with gilded Tudor-style moldings. Textured paper on the ceiling creates opacity and depth, and forms a dramatic backdrop for a chandelier from Marvin Alexander. PHOTOGRAPHY BY BILLY CUNNINGHAM

Rich oak paneling and a textural low-relief plaster ceiling established the tone for this English Tudor library by Ann W. Platz of ANN PLATZ & COMPANY. Produced for the DECORATORS' SHOW HOUSE in Atlanta, Georgia, the room is defined by a custom carpet, an adaptation of an Aubusson found at the Georgia Governor's Mansion. Textiles were chosen in a range of colors—raisin, aubergine, garnet and natural linen—found in the carpet. A chinoiserie secretary and a collection of Imari porcelain are examples of the many Asian decorative touches.

PHOTOGRAPHY BY PRO STUDIO, ATLANTA

ABOVE LEFT

David L. Scott of DAVID SCOTT INTERIORS, LTD. designed a sitting room extension of a master bedroom suite for empty nesters who have condensed their former living space into a comfortable condominium apartment. At the ANSONIA CONDOMINIUM SHOWCASE in New York City, he used a mix of clean-lined beige velvet armchairs and an impressive collection of 19th-century European antiques, giving the space a modern attitude without losing its sense of heritage.

PHOTOGRAPHY BY TIM LEE

RIGHT

The inviting nature of this attractive retreat at the OAK & IVY SHOW HOUSE AND GARDEN in Montclair, New Jersey, comes from an eclectic mix of period furnishings. Designer Mark A. Polo of POLO M.A., INC. combined Art Deco with 18th-century French and 19th-century Chinese pieces to create an intimate salon with old-world elegance. The soothing walls, upholstered in Swiss wool, create a feeling of uniformity with the window treatments— layers of wool puddled loosely over silk plaid. All fabrics are from Kirk Brummel.   PHOTOGRAPHY BY PETER PAIGE

In the Tudor home of the PASADENA SHOWCASE HOUSE OF DESIGN in California, Billy W. Francis and Ed Russell of FRANCIS-RUSSELL DESIGN-DECORATION, INC. softened a dark wood paneled corner with a plump silk sofa and grand verdure tapestry. A graceful pedestal table and significant Biedermeier chest, polished to reveal a rich patina, imbue the space with warmth and elegance.   PHOTOGRAPHY BY MARTIN FINE PHOTOGRAPHY

OPPOSITE

A sleeping car of the Orient Express was the inspiration for a small sitting room by designer Jennifer Garrigues of JENNIFER GARRIGUES, INC. for the KIPS BAY BOYS & GIRLS CLUB DECORATOR SHOW HOUSE in New York City. In this tiny jewel box, Garrigues illustrates how a small space can contain practical storage solutions and possess enormous exotic appeal. Her brilliant ensemble of antiques, textures and light play, sets the stage for a welcoming oasis. PHOTOGRAPHY BY MATTIELLO/STEELE ASSOCIATES

ABOVE LEFT & RIGHT

An awkward upstairs servant's room was turned into a stylish study in the SAN FRANCISCO UNIVERSITY HIGH SCHOOL DECORATORS' SHOWCASE in California. In order to emphasize the spectacular view of San Francisco Bay, designer Anne Marie Vingo of ANNE MARIE VINGO INTERIOR DESIGN widened the arched window and built a comfortable window seat with storage compartments and accented with rich jewel-toned pillows. The neoclassic desk is punctuated by black and white accessories. Behind it, a tall aerial map folding screen softens an angled wall. A closet was removed to make way for a work space with counters, drawers, and shelves. PHOTOGRAPHY BY DAVID DUNCAN LIVINGSTON

LEFT

At the KIPS BAY BOYS & GIRLS CLUB DECORATOR SHOW HOUSE in New York City, a tiny study originally installed by acclaimed architect Philip Johnson in 1931-1932, was updated in a sophisticated modernist style by William T. Georgis of WILLIAM T. GEORGIS, ARCHITECT. Georgis kept Johnson's streamlined wood cabinetry and paneling but covered the original plaster walls with brushed stainless steel, providing a cool counterpoint to the warm wood. Crushed velvet drapes and a nickel and polyester shade are bold accents.

PHOTOGRAPHY BY T. WHITNEY COX

Designed by Wendy Reynolds of CHEEVER HOUSE for the JUNIOR LEAGUE OF BOSTON DECORATORS' SHOWHOUSE in Massachusetts, this refined home office exemplifies casual elegance set within a traditional framework. Her goal was to create an uncluttered, personal work space for the woman of the house, using comfortable furnishings and fine fabrics. A French writing desk provides decorative allure. PHOTOGRAPHY BY © SAM GRAY

RIGHT

A pastoral mural sets the stage for this fanciful child's storybook hideaway in a turn-of-the-century mansion that was once home to Woodrow Wilson. The room, designed by Corinne Lalin, Mark Pettegrow, and John Schmidtberger of BRUSHWORKS, INC. for the JUNIOR LEAGUE OF GREATER PRINCETON SHOWHOUSE in New Jersey, was inspired by the tales of Beatrix Potter. The children of the house can spend an afternoon at play on the trompe l'oeil floorcloth created by the designers. PHOTOGRAPHY BY RANDL BYE

Beth Rodewig of RODEWIG RE-DECORATING/DECORATIVE PAINTING AND DETAILS hand stenciled graceful flowers and climbing vines on the walls as well as on the demi-lune table in this imaginary ladies' morning room for the DESIGNER'S SHOWHOUSE XII in Centerville, Massachusetts. One Art Deco inspired chair stands alone in this private retreat.   PHOTOGRAPHY BY RANDALL PERRY PHOTOGRAPHY

RIGHT

Thomas Jayne of THOMAS JAYNE STUDIO, INC. wanted to evoke the comfort of an Edwardian morning room for the KIPS BAY BOYS & GIRLS CLUB DECORATOR SHOW HOUSE in New York City. Here one can read the newspaper in plump, cushioned chairs, eat breakfast at the table or peruse the morning mail on the cherry secretary from Bernard & S. Dean Levy, Inc. A soft toned color palette was dictated by the Turkish carpet which is from Doris Leslie Blau, Inc.

PHOTOGRAPHY BY DUB ROGERS

BELOW LEFT & RIGHT

In a restful palette of ochre and umber, Laurie J. Steichen of STEICHEN INTERIOR DESIGN, INC. enveloped a quiet upstairs retreat off the front balcony of the JUNIOR LEAGUE OF NEW ORLEANS DECORATORS' SHOW HOUSE VIII in Louisiana. To endow the room with a grand and glamorous aura, the designer placed tall panels of aged mirrors and gilded moldings around the space. To further accentuate the room's height, she set an 18th-century French Regency sofa beneath a drape of wispy sun-faded linen. A pair of worn French leather club chairs with velvet seat cushions flanks an old cricket table in front of the marble fireplace.

PHOTOGRAPHY BY KERRI MCCAFFETY

Suzanne Kasler Morris of SUZANNE KASLER INTERIORS adopted an elegant European approach for the loggia of the DECORATORS' SHOW HOUSE in Atlanta, Georgia, which she envisioned as the perfect spot for afternoon tea. The ethereal blue ceiling mural, painted years ago, inspired Kasler to wash the walls in welcoming periwinkle blue. Gold paint was used to define the arched doorways, and a French mirror contributes to the room's symmetry by reflecting columns on the opposite wall. PHOTOGRAPHY BY © ROBERT THIEN

Designer Daniel Mullay of BLOOMINGDALE'S re-created a floral garden in a lady's dressing room for the ESTATE AND GARDENS AT BEL AIR SHOWHOUSE in Livingston, New Jersey. He used a soft palette of pink, aqua, and sky blue, offset against a bold Chinese carpet. Brightly colored plaid taffeta from Brunschwig & Fils covers two heart-shaped slipper chairs.   PHOTOGRAPHY BY BILL ROTHSCHILD

The design concept maintained by Gerald C. Tolomeo of GERALD C. TOLOMEO LTD. is "to use unexpected elements within a single space and . . . add accessories that make you smile." His sunny upstairs lair at the ROGERS MEMORIAL LIBRARY DESIGNERS' SHOWHOUSE in Southampton, New York, achieved a relaxed look by combining traditional well-bred furnishings with contemporary designs. A zebra-striped table gives the stately sofa and antique pine secretary a whimsical jolt.   PHOTOGRAPHY BY ALEC HEMER

Sig Bergamin of SIG BERGAMIN ARQUITETURA was inspired by the colors and style of the Caribbean Islands when he created this sitting room for CASA COR in São Paulo, Brazil. A blue and white palette suggests beach house informality. Seaside photographs, birdcages, and lush orchids define the theme of this tropical solarium.
PHOTOGRAPHY BY TUCA REINÉS

At the PASADENA SHOWCASE HOUSE OF DESIGN in California, Lisa K. Jackson and Dominique Sardell of L.K.J. INTERIORS created a retreat in the basement of a Tudor-style mansion, despite limitations of its windowless architecture. This softly lit music room replaces sunshine with lambent lighting. The designers' use of Tuscan colors is evident in the antique rugs, paisley armchairs and suede bergères.   PHOTOGRAPHY BY DAVID GLOMB

Designed by Mario Buatta of MARIO BUATTA INTERIOR DESIGN for the KIPS BAY BOYS & GIRLS CLUB DECORATOR SHOW HOUSE in New York City, a verdant garden room is embraced by a panoply of patterns in bright jewel tones. A soft chinoiserie mural forms an ethereal backdrop to the designer's signature showpiece of casual English country style. PHOTOGRAPHY REPRINTED BY PERMISSION FROM *HOUSE BEAUTIFUL*, COPYRIGHT © SEPTEMBER, 1997. HEARST COMMUNICATIONS, INC. ALL RIGHTS RESERVED. THIBAULT JEANSON, PHOTOGRAPHER

ABOVE LEFT & RIGHT

For the stately Gothic Revival mansion housing the HUDSON RIVER DESIGNER SHOWHOUSE in South Nyack, New York, designer Patricia Kocak of PATRICIA KOCAK INTERIORS was assigned the verandas adjacent to the main entry portico. For the largest veranda, multiple seating arrangements were created by utilizing her collection of antique wicker furniture. Plaid cotton awning shades were hung between the columns and the wainscoted ceiling was painted in a coordinating pale green tone. Original wooden floors were faux painted in a diamond pattern resembling vintage slate. In a corner of another outdoor porch sits a custom-designed rustic stone table where cast-iron chairs and a Victorian wire bench are employed for alfresco meals. PHOTOGRAPHY BY © PHILLIP ENNIS

RIGHT

At the PHILHARMONIC HOUSE OF DESIGN in San Juan Capistrano, California, natural canvas panels frame views of the picturesque surroundings. Designers Robert Esterley and Jill Scheetz of ESTERLEY-SCHEETZ & ASSOCIATES, INC. provided visual interest to a long, narrow upstairs veranda by creating an inviting sitting room amidst a terrace garden. Smith & Hawken outdoor furniture blends with statuesque stone planters.

PHOTOGRAPHY BY A.G. PHOTOGRAPHY

Jamie Gibbs of JAMIE GIBBS AND ASSOCIATES set the stage for an exotic Roman bath in the sunroom of the SHOWHOUSE AT THE SHORE in Ventnor, New Jersey. Gibbs draped the windows and skylights with billowing silk panels to evoke a Roman campaign tent setting. Lush foliage, including orchids, cyclamens and tropical trees, thrive in the humid environment. Jewel-toned tiles, faux marble, and gold leaf add to the room's exotic appeal.

PHOTOGRAPHY BY BILL ROTHSCHILD

High above the busy streets of San Francisco, a calm sanctuary was created by landscape designer Matthew Schoenwald of CALYPSO LANDSCAPE. The pleasing serenity of his terrace garden at the SAN FRANCISCO UNIVERSITY HIGH SCHOOL DECORATORS' SHOWCASE in California is achieved through sculptural forms, running water, and sensitivity to the breathtaking panorama. A glass wind partition is fronted by ornamental grasses and a container garden.

PHOTOGRAPHY BY DAVID DUNCAN LIVINGSTON

Designers Richard A. Cannon and Richard P. Bullock of CANNON/BULLOCK knew the owners of the house which presented the SHOWCASE HOUSE OF DESIGN in Toluca Lake, California, and of their desire for a pool house where they could essentially live all summer. A covered dining area and bar lead out to the poolside where the deck and interior spaces were unified with practical slate tile. Chinese accessories and tables contribute to the Asian flavor set amidst the soft summer color scheme of eggplant, celadon and creamy beige. Contemporary, yet classic furniture is made of teak from Summit and fabrics from Sunbrella are easily cleaned and durable in all weather.

PHOTOGRAPHY BY © CAMERON CAROTHERS PHOTOGRAPHY

Ancient wisteria forms a magical canopy over a narrow terrace behind the DECORATORS' SHOWHOUSE & GARDEN TOUR in Lakewood, Washington. DeAnne D. Brenneis of THE JOHN BRENNEIS ARCHITECTS arranged casual outdoor furniture around brightly colored ceramic containers and lifelike animal topiaries. The daybed and chairs are woven from Thailand's plentiful water hyacinth plants. PHOTOGRAPHY BY PATRICIA RUSH, CREATIVE EDGE PHOTOGRAPHY STUDIO

A splash garden to surround an existing swimming pool at the OAK & IVY SHOW HOUSE AND GARDEN in Montclair, New Jersey, was designed by Brian J. Koribanick of LANDSCAPE TECHNIQUES INC. Cobblestone pavers were used in the patio to integrate the architecture of the home with the garden. The gazebo and teak garden furniture are joined by graceful borders of sun and shade plants. PHOTOGRAPHY BY © IMAGE/DENNIS KRUKOWSKI

A sunny terrace featuring tropical foliage and vibrant yellow cushions brightens the back garden of the CRI•DESIGNER SHOW HOUSE in New York City. Jamie Gibbs of JAMIE GIBBS AND ASSOCIATES installed a large retractable awning to create an all-weather entertaining space. Red wooden conga drums, used as drink tables, add another touch of the tropics.

PHOTOGRAPHY BY TIM EBERT PHOTOGRAPHY

Early 20th-century Tudor style homes often had second story sleeping porches, as did this mansion that hosted the JUNIOR LEAGUE OF GREATER PRINCETON SHOWHOUSE in New Jersey. Bruce Long and Robert Giberson of BRUCE NORMAN LONG converted it to a private breakfast retreat, replete with comfortable weatherproof chairs and chaise. To be compatible with the spirit of the black timber and white stucco home, the designers draped black latticework with white netting to camouflage the screens.

PHOTOGRAPHY BY MELABEE M. MILLER

ABOVE LEFT & RIGHT

Architect Donald Beck of BECK ARCHITECTURE, INC. followed the adage, "You never get a second chance to make a first impression," when he designed the front porch of the ULTIMATE SHOWHOUSE in Cincinnati, Ohio. Combining crisp awning stripes and cool verdant colors, he created an inviting space that beckons the guest to linger awhile. The architect designed the floor, a bold grid of German limestone, English bluestone, and Italian marble, to anchor a granite topped table. A Niermann Weeks chandelier casts an amber glow on a sculptural antique English finial.

PHOTOGRAPHY BY J. MILES WOLF ©1997

LEFT

Designers Patricia Bonis and Michael Mariotti of BONIS/MARIOTTI & ASSOCIATES were influenced by nature when they created this ocean terrace of the SPRING LAKE SHOWHOUSE in New Jersey. A palette of colors from the sea and sky reflects the exquisite view which is softened by tumbling fishnet shades.

PHOTOGRAPHY BY GEORGE ROSS

ABOVE

The solarium designed by Rena Fortgang of RENA FORTGANG INTERIOR DESIGNS, INC. for the MANSIONS & MILLIONAIRES DESIGNERS' SHOWCASE in Lattingtown, New York is crisply underscored by a blue and white color scheme. Just off the swimming pool, this indoor/outdoor room is encircled by a wall of tall windows accentuated by an awning striped valance and several floor to ceiling drapes. A cozy and informal spot for lunch is provided by a cherry French provincial dining table. PHOTOGRAPHY BY © PHILLIP ENNIS

LEFT & RIGHT

Landscape architect, Joan E. Furlong of JOAN E. FURLONG, LANDSCAPE ARCHITECT, reconfigured the backyard of the OAK & IVY SHOW HOUSE AND GARDEN in Montclair, New Jersey, into a child's magical wonderland. Part maze, part fun house, part edible garden—this is a veritable field of dreams. PHOTOGRAPHY BY © IMAGE/DENNIS KRUKOWSKI

Michaela Scherrer of MICHAELA SCHERRER & ASSOCIATES created a wonderfully soothing and modern oasis for the senses in the PASADENA SHOWCASE HOUSE OF DESIGN in California. Using aromatherapy, incense, and water as design elements, she transformed the veranda into a private meditative retreat. The acid-washed scored concrete floor is a cool counterpoint to the greenery and motion of the water garden. PHOTOGRAPHY BY MICHAEL E. GARLAND

Rena Fortgang of RENA FORTGANG INTERIOR DESIGNS, INC. fused old-world elegance with country charm in her "getaway veranda" at the DECORATOR SHOWHOUSE in Oyster Bay, New York. Weather treated white drapes are elegantly tied back in each archway to catch the breeze. By combining French country antiques with rustic twig furniture, she created an airy respite and a quiet spot for dinner à deux. PHOTOGRAPHY BY BILL ROTHSCHILD

Ed Russell of FRANCIS-RUSSELL DESIGN-DECORATION, INC. created a practical and sophisticated outdoor room for the PASADENA SHOWCASE HOUSE OF DESIGN in California. The furniture, crafted of teakwood, is by Summit. Striped cushions are made of awning fabric and waterproofed. The light fixtures were influenced by Japanese lanterns. PHOTOGRAPHY BY MARTIN FINE PHOTOGRAPHY

Ann Beard Interiors
Ann Beard
2000 Richard Jones Road
Nashville, Tennessee 37215
Tel: (615) 297-9484
Fax: (615) 297-9397

Ann Platz & Company
Ann W. Platz, IIDA
5 Piedmont Center
Atlanta, Georgia 30305
Tel: (404) 237-1000
Fax: (404) 237-3810

Anne Cooper Interiors, Inc.
Anne Cooper
80 Clark Road
Bernardsville, New Jersey 07960
Tel: (908) 696-0464
Fax: (908) 696-0490

Anne Marie Vingo Interior Design
Anne Marie Vingo
2565 California Street
San Francisco, California 94115
Tel: (415) 776-7555
Fax: (415) 776-7693

Anne Zuckerberg Associates
Anne Zuckerberg
Elise Kodish
2055 Center Avenue
Fort Lee, New Jersey 07024
Tel/Fax: (201) 592-7257

Antine Associates, Inc.
Anthony Antine
Ho Sang Shin
750 Park Avenue
New York, New York 10021
Tel: (212) 988-4096
Fax: (201) 941-9250

Antiquariato
Hicham O. Ghandour
150 West 28th Street
New York, New York 10001
Tel: (212) 727-0733

Artistic Designs
Carol Huber
68 Sunset Avenue
Verona, New Jersey 07044
Tel: (973) 239-2271
Fax: (973) 731-7790

Barbara Hauben-Ross, Inc.
Barbara Hauben-Ross
Lauder Bowden
226 East 54th Street
New York, New York 10022
Tel: (212) 832-6640
Fax: (212) 421-3358

Barbara Ostrom Associates, Inc.
Barbara Ostrom
1 International Boulevard
Mahwah, New Jersey 07495
Tel: (201) 529-0444
Fax: (201) 529-0449

Barbara Pelly Associates
Barbara Pelly
651 Northumberland Road
Teaneck, New Jersey 07666
Tel: (201) 836-5276
Fax: (201) 928-4173

Bebe Winkler Interior Design, Inc.
Bebe Winkler
969 Third Avenue
New York, New York 10022
Tel: (212) 838-3356
Fax: (212) 223-4977

Beck Architecture, Inc.
Donald Beck, AIA
550 Liberty Hill
Cincinnati, Ohio 45210
Tel: (513) 651-5550
Fax: (513) 721-2648

Beverly Ellsley Design
Beverly Ellsley
179 Post Road West
Westport, Connecticut 06880
Tel: (203) 227-1157
Fax: (203) 227-6681

Bierly-Drake Associates, Inc.
Lee Bierly, ASID
Christopher Drake, ASID
17 Arlington Street
Boston, Massachusetts 02116
Tel: (617) 247-0081
Fax: (617) 247-6395

Bloomingdale's
Daniel Mullay
The Mall at Short Hills
Short Hills, New Jersey 07078
Tel: (973) 548-2416
Fax: (973) 548-2206

Blue Skies
Morrene Jacobs
174 Springfield Avenue
Summit, New Jersey 07901
Tel: (908) 273-4512
Fax: (908) 598-9402

Bonis/Mariotti & Associates
Patricia Bonis
Michael Mariotti
8 Fairway Court
Cresskill, New Jersey 07626
Tel: (201) 894-9082
Fax: (201) 894-1266

Boxwood House, Inc.
Melinda Johnson
Michael Johnson
27 Woodland Park Drive
Tenafly, New Jersey 07670
Tel: (201) 871-3323
Fax: (201) 871-1187

Bruce Norman Long
Bruce Long
Robert Giberson
344 Nassau Street
Princeton, New Jersey 08540
Tel: (609) 921-1401
Fax: (609) 921-3248

**Brunete Fraccaroli Arquitetura e
Interiores**
Brunete Fraccaroli
Rua Guarará 261/7°
São Paulo, São Paulo 01425001
Brazil
Tel: (55) 11-885-8309
Fax: (55) 11-887-6834

Brushworks, Inc.
Corinne Lalin
Mark Pettegrow
John Schmidtberger
P.O. Box 484
New Hope, Pennsylvania 18938
Tel: (215) 598-3318
Fax: (215) 598-8181
www.brushworks.com

Calypso Landscape
Matthew Schoenwald
6 Vallejo Street
Berkeley, California 94707
Tel: (510) 527-8600
Fax: (510) 528-9022

Cannon/Bullock
Richard A. Cannon
Richard P. Bullock
9903 Santa Monica Boulevard
Beverly Hills, California 90212
Tel: (213) 221-9286
Fax: (213) 221-9287

Castles Interiors
Pam Kelker
85 South Union Boulevard
Lakewood, Colorado 80228
Tel: (303) 989-0801
Fax: (303) 980-0040

Catherine Gerry Interiors
Catherine Gerry
302 West 98th Street
New York, New York 10025
Tel: (212) 663-5466
Fax: (212) 749-9097

Cheever House
Wendy Reynolds
14 Cheever Circle
Andover, Massachusetts 01810
Tel: (978) 875-4931
Fax: (978) 475-2082

Cheryl Womack Interiors
Cheryl Womack
4110 Thunderbird Drive
Marietta, Georgia 30067
Tel: (770) 951-0285
Fax: (770) 226-0126

**Christine Hawley Custom Wine Cellar
Design with Sherry-Lehman, Inc.**
Christine Hawley
155 West 70th Street
New York, New York 10023
Tel: (212) 721-0831
Fax: (212) 721-0853

Claudia Aquino Interiors
Claudia Aquino
3955 Northside Drive
Atlanta, Georgia 30342
Tel: (404) 266-9983
Fax: (404) 233-1242

Collections II
Kathy Slater, ASID
3901 Magazine Street
New Orleans, Louisiana 70115
Tel: (504) 895-7375
Fax: (504) 528-1030

Courland Design Inc.
Mercedes Courland
708 Glen Cove Avenue
Glen Head, New York 11545
Tel: (516) 759-4802
Fax: (516) 671-8589

Crilly Companies
Maureen Crilly
211 West 61st Street
New York, New York 10023
Tel: (212) 489-4752
Fax: (212) 489-4855

Cynthia Bennett & Associates, Inc.
Cynthia F. Bennett
501 Fair Oaks Avenue
South Pasadena, California 91030
Tel: (626) 799-9701
Fax: (626) 799-9716

David Kaplan Interior Design
David Kaplan
290 West 12th Street
New York, New York 10014
Tel: (212) 462-4329
Fax: (212) 462-4399

David Scott Interiors, Ltd.
David L. Scott, Allied ASID
151 East 80th Street
New York, New York 10021
Tel/Fax: (212) 988-3620

de Quesada Architects, Inc.
Jorge de Quesada
447 Pacific Avenue
San Francisco, California 94133
Tel: (415) 434-3691
Fax: (415) 434-3694

Design I
Marilee Schempp, ASID
497 Springfield Avenue
Summit, New Jersey 07901
Tel: (908) 277-1110
Fax: (908) 277-0154

Design Source
Alix Rico
Patricia Brinson
115 Fairway Drive
New Orleans, Louisiana 70124
Tel: (504) 488-0205
Fax: (504) 482-7476

**Douglas Wilson Ltd., Decorative
Painting**
Douglas Wilson
1495 Third Avenue
New York, New York 10028
Tel: (212) 794-0896
Fax: (212) 794-9177

Drake Design Associates, Inc.
Jamie Drake, ASID
140 East 56th Street
New York, New York 10022
Tel: (212) 754-3099
Fax: (212) 754-4389

East End Interiors
Rosalba Campitiello
William Johnson
4832 Sunrise Highway
Sayville, New York 11782
Tel: (516) 567-5001
Fax: (516) 567-5011

Entasis
Eugene Perreault
109 East Patrick Street
Frederick, Maryland 21701
Tel: (301) 607-0152
Fax: (301) 682-6175

Esterley-Scheetz & Associates, Inc.
Robert Esterley, Allied ASID
Jill Scheetz, Allied ASID
2711 East Coast Highway
Corona del Mar, California 92625
Tel: (714) 673-5595
Fax: (714) 673-5598

Euro Concepts, Ltd.
Sari Feuer
Stephen Kazantzis
1802 Jericho Turnpike
Huntington, New York 11743
Tel: (516) 493-0983
Fax: (516) 493-0986

**Francis C. Klein and Associates,
Architects**
Francis C. Klein
Gottfried Bierbacher
Maria Bucci
484 Bloomfield Avenue
Montclair, New Jersey 07042
Tel: (973) 783-0688
Fax: (973) 783-3010

Francis-Russell Design-Decoration, Inc.
Billy W. Francis
Ed Russell
800 Fifth Avenue
New York, New York 10021
Tel: (212) 832-8404
Fax: (212) 980-4842

Freya Surabian Design Associates
Freya Surabian
36 Church Street
Winchester, Massachusetts 01890
Tel: (781) 729-4911
Fax: (781) 729-3494

Gabberts Furniture & Design Studio
Carole Smith Harston, ASID
Marie Hayden, ASID
6301 Oakmont Boulevard
Fort Worth, Texas 76132
Tel: (817) 346-5660
Fax: (817) 346-5665

Geoffrey Bradfield Inc.
Geoffrey N. Bradfield
105 East 63rd Street
New York, New York 10021
Tel: (212) 758-1773
Fax: (212) 688-1571

Gerald C. Tolomeo Ltd.
Gerald C. Tolomeo
96 Rockland Avenue
Little Falls, New Jersey 07424
Tel: (913) 742-8520
Fax: (913) 742-9404

Geri's Creative Imagery
Geri Loudenslager
2926 Sunrise Avenue
Bristol, Pennsylvania 19007
Tel: (215) 785-4398
Fax: (215) 785-2243

Glenn Lawson, Inc.
Glenn Lawson
240 Central Park South
New York, New York 10019
Fax/Tel: (212) 586-5646

**Green & Company, Inc. Interior
Designers**
Gail Green
110 East 59th Street
New York, New York 10022
Tel: (212) 909-0396
Fax: (212) 909-0377

Greg Lanza Interior Design
Greg Lanza
60 Forest Avenue
Locust Valley, New York 11560
Tel: (516) 671-6028
Fax: (516) 671-4282

Hammer & Schmidt Design
Peggy Hammerschmidt
P.O. Box 7728
Aspen, Colorado 81612
Tel: (970) 544-5757
Fax: (970) 544-5775

Hendrixson's Furniture
Noreen Dunn
Sally Dunn
P.O. Box 335
Furlong, Pennsylvania 18925
Tel: (215) 794-7325
Fax: (215) 794-0983

Imagination Unlimited
Lorraine Volz
43 Page Drive
Hicksville, New York 11801
Tel: (516) 935-7235

Interior Accents
Cynthia Kasper, ASID
43 Farview Farm Road
West Redding, Connecticut 06896
Tel: (203) 938-3010
Fax: (203) 938-3314

Interior Design Solutions, Inc.
Susan Aiello, ASID
300 East 74th Street
New York, New York 10021
Tel/Fax: (212) 628-3938

Interior Options
Michael Love, ASID
200 Lexington Avenue
New York, New York 10016
Tel: (212) 545-0301
Fax: (212) 689-4064

The Interior Shop
Linda Delier
Richard Delier
James Gill
Route 202
Buckingham, Pennsylvania 18912
Tel: (215) 794-2266
Fax: (215) 794-2242

J. Murray Vise Interior Design
J. Murray Vise, IIDA
808 Argonne Avenue NE
Atlanta, Georgia 30308
Tel: (404) 892-9708

Jackie Naylor Interiors Inc.
Jackie Naylor, ASID, CKD, CBD
Kathleen Beres, Allied ASID
4287 Glengary Drive NE
Atlanta, Georgia 30342
Tel/Fax: (404) 814-1973

Jacqueline's Interior Design Studio, Inc.
Jacqueline Epstein, Allied ASID
Barclay Pavilion
Cherry Hill, New Jersey 08034
Tel: (609) 216-1110
Fax: (609) 216-0666

James Rixner Inc.
James Rixner, ASID
121 Morton Street
New York, New York 10014
Tel: (212) 206-7439
Fax: (212) 206-6636

Jamie Gibbs and Associates
Jamie Gibbs, ASID, IFDA
340 East 93rd Street
New York, New York 10128
Tel: (212) 722-7508
Fax: (212) 369-6332

Jeannie McKeogh Interiors
Jeannie McKeogh
410 Vincent Avenue
Metairie, Louisiana 70005
Tel: (504) 837-1382
Fax: (504) 833-7097

Jennifer Garrigues, Inc.
Jennifer Garrigues
Allison Paladino
Margaret Poetz
308 Peruvian Avenue
Palm Beach, Florida 33480
Tel: (561) 659-7085
Fax: (561) 659-7090

Joan E. Furlong, Landscape Architect
Joan E. Furlong, ASLA, CLA
39 Norman Road
Montclair, New Jersey 07043
Tel: (973) 744-6687
Fax: (973) 743-7139

Joel Allen
229 East 79th Street
New York, New York 10021
Tel/Fax: (212) 744-7952

Johansen Interiors
Joan Johansen
Lisa McTernan
424 Central Avenue
Peekskill, New York 10566
Tel: (914) 739-6293

The John Brenneis Architects
DeAnne D. Brenneis, IIDA
6064 Second Avenue NW
Seattle, Washington 98107
Tel: (206) 784-3626
Fax: (206) 781-0829

John A. Buscarello, Inc.
John A. Buscarello, ASID
27 West 20th Street
New York, New York 10011
Tel: (212) 691-5881
Fax: (212) 691-5916

John Kelly Interior Design, Inc.
John Kelly, ASID
2031 Locust Street
Philadelphia, Pennsylvania 19103
Tel: (215) 557-7668
Fax: (215) 557-7666

Johnny Grey and Company, USA
Johnny Grey
Joan Picone
49A Route 202
Far Hills, New Jersey 07931
Tel: (908) 781-1554
Fax: (908) 781-1543

K-II Designs, Ltd.
Diane Knight
111 121 Birch Hill Road
Locust Valley, New York 11560
Tel: (516) 671-7046
Fax: (516) 759-0059

Kathryne Designs
Kathryne A. Dahlman, ASID
4442 Gentry Avenue
North Hollywood, California 91607
Tel: (818) 762-3705
Fax: (818) 760-2640

KFD Designs, Ltd.
Kimberley Fiterman, ASID
60 West 12th Street
New York, New York 10011
Tel: (212) 633-0660
Fax: (212) 675-1097

Kurt Cyr Interior Design & Decoration
Kurt Cyr
6840 Claire Avenue
Reseda, California 91335
Tel: (818) 881-0006
Fax: (818) 881-0362

Landscape Techniques Inc.
Brian J. Koribanick
187 Washington Avenue
Nutley, New Jersey 07110
Tel: (973) 667-8050
Fax: (973) 667-0845

Lawrence Design
Larry Froemmling
24552 Via Del Oro
Laguna Niguel, California 92677
Tel: (714) 643-3434
Fax: (714) 643-1930

LeAnne Tamaribuchi Interior Design
LeAnne Tamaribuchi, ASID, CID
Cheryl Rader
1 Sunlight
Irvine, California 92612
Tel: (714) 854-7061
Fax: (714) 854-8160

Leruth Interior Design
Kay Leruth, ASID, CID
21672 Cabrosa Street
Mission Viejo, California 92691
Tel: (714) 454-2939
Fax: (714) 829-8255

Letelier & Rock Design, Inc.
Jorge Letelier
Sheryl Asklund Rock
1020 Madison Avenue
New York, New York 10021
Tel: (212) 683-5512
Fax: (212) 683-7608

L.K.J. Interiors
Lisa K. Jackson
Dominique Sardell
291 South Glenroy Avenue
Los Angeles, California 90049
Tel: (310) 471-5585
Fax: (310) 476-1776

Locust Valley Design Center
Jacqueline Ann Cappa
John Cappa, Jr.
50 Forest Avenue
Locust Valley, New York 11560
Tel: (516) 676-0760
Fax: (718) 850-3488

Lynne Herman Interiors
Lynne Herman
20161 Palm Island Drive
Boca Raton, Florida 33498
Tel: (561) 883-0070
Fax: (561) 883-0066

Margaret Donaldson Interiors
Margaret Donaldson, ASID
284-A Meeting Street
Charleston, South Carolina 29401
Tel: (803) 722-2640
Fax: (803) 722-7901

Marilyn Katz Interior Design, Ltd.
Marilyn Katz
630 Park Avenue
New York, New York 10021
Tel: (212) 535-0318

Mario Buatta Interior Design
Mario Buatta
120 East 80th Street
New York, New York 10021
Tel: (212) 988-6811
Fax: (212) 861-9321

Mario Villa, Inc.
Mario Villa
3908 Magazine Street
New Orleans, Louisiana 70115
Tel: (504) 895 8731
Fax: (504) 895-7431

Marjorie Stark Interior Design
Marjorie Stark
5671 South Nevada
Littleton, Colorado 80120
Tel: (303) 347-8961
Fax: (303) 347-8974

Marshall Watson Interiors, Ltd.
Marshall Watson
462 West 52nd Street
New York, New York 10019
Tel: (212) 664-8094
Fax: (212) 582-4364

McMillen, Inc.
Katherine McCallum
Priscilla Ulmann
155 East 56th Street
New York, New York 10022
Tel: (212) 753-5600
Fax: (212) 759-7563

Michael Carey Interior Design, Inc.
Michael Carey
1854 Pacific Coast Highway
Laguna Beach, California 92651
Tel: (714) 376-9876
Fax: (714) 376-5507

Michael de Santis, Inc.
Michael de Santis, ASID
1110 Second Avenue
New York, New York 10022
Tel: (212) 753-8871
Fax: (212) 935-7777

Michael Mariotti Interior Design
Michael M. Mariotti
13 Jay Street
Tenafly, New Jersey 07670
Tel: (201) 568-9551
Fax: (201) 568-9553

Michael Simon Interiors, Inc.
Michael Simon
180 West 58th Street
New York, New York 10019
Tel: (212) 307-7670
Fax: (212) 307-0742

Michael Tyson Murphy Studio
Michael Tyson Murphy
135 West 20th Street
New York, New York 10011
Tel: (212) 989-0180
Fax: (212) 989-0443

Michaela Scherrer & Associates
Michaela Scherrer
54 West Colorado Boulevard
Pasadena, California 91105
Tel: (626) 449-1242
Fax: (626) 449-5142

Myles Scott Harlan Interior Design
Myles Scott Harlan
45 Tudor City Place
New York, New York 10017
Tel: (212) 661-3930
Fax: (212) 661-7597

Norman Michaeloff Interior Design, Inc.
Norman Michaeloff
177 East 75th Street
New York, New York 10021
Tel/Fax: (212) 288-5400

Ogawa/Depardon Architects
Kathryn Ogawa
Gilles Depardon
137 Varick Street
New York, New York 10013
Tel: (212) 627-7390
Fax: (212) 627-9681

Orsini Design Associates
Susan Orsini
330 East 59th Street
New York, New York 10022
Tel: (212) 371-8400
Fax: (212) 935-8615

Pamela Copeman Interiors
Pamela Copeman
1 Fulling Mill Lane
Hingham, Massachusetts 02043
Tel: (617) 749-0581

Patricia Bonis Interiors, Inc.
Patricia Bonis
979 Third Avenue
New York, New York 10021
Tel: (212) 980-6040
Fax: (212) 980-4760

Patricia Kocak Interiors
Patricia Kocak
202 Lexow Avenue
Upper Nyack, New York 10960
Tel/Fax: (914) 358-8805

Pensis-Stolz Inc.
Albert E. Pensis
200 Lexington Avenue
New York, New York 10016
Tel: (212) 686-1788
Fax: (212) 689-2982

Peter Charles Associates, Ltd.
Peter Charles Lopipero
17 East Main Street
Oyster Bay, New York 11771
Tel: (516) 624-9276
Fax: (516) 624-9367

Phyllis Avant Interiors, Inc.
Phyllis K. Avant, ASID
Tisha Borders, Allied ASID
3503 Murphy Road
Nashville, Tennessee 37205
Tel: (615) 383-7070
Fax: (615) 383-3568

piadesign inc.
Pia Ledy
120 East 57th Street
New York, New York 10022
Tel: (212) 486-2021
Fax: (212) 486-2031

Piller Design
Kara Piller, Allied ASID
28241 Crown Valley Parkway
Laguna Niguel, California 92677
Tel: (714) 470-0280
Fax: (714) 348-7024

Polo M.A., Inc.
Mark A. Polo
1107 Buckingham Road
Fort Lee, New Jersey 07024
Tel: (201) 224-0322
Fax: (201) 224-0150

Quattro Canti Interiors
Karen Padgett Prewitt, Allied ASID
33 Hasell Street
Charleston, South Carolina 29401
Tel: (803) 722-8125
Fax: (803) 853-6872

R. Scott Lalley Interior Design
Scott Lalley
Raymond J. Cuminale
200 Central Park South
New York, New York 10019
Tel/Fax: (212) 265-4333

Rare Bits
Sherry McFadden
Andrée Lago
800 Metairie Road
Metairie, Louisiana 70005
Tel: (504) 837-6771

Regency Kitchens, Inc.
Rochelle Kalisch
4204 14th Avenue
Brooklyn, New York 11219
Tel: (718) 435-4266
Fax: (718) 435-5411

Regina T. Kraft
477 Woodbury Road
Cold Spring Harbor, New York 11724
Tel: (516) 692-6278
Fax: (516) 692-7426

Rena Fortgang Interior Designs, Inc.
Rena Fortgang, Assoc., ASID
27 Forest Avenue
Locust Valley, New York 11560
Tel: (516) 759-7826
Fax: (516) 759-7828

Renwick Design
Gwynneth R. Davis
6292 Ingham Road
New Hope, Pennsylvania 18938
Tel/Fax: (215) 862-0830

Reusser Bergstrom Associates
Marc Reusser
Debra Bergstrom
465 South El Molino Avenue
Pasadena, California 91101
Tel: (626) 577-9088
Fax: (626) 577-1038

Retorno Estudio
Cynthia De Winne
Andres Levy
Juan Alvarez Morales
Arroyo 873
Buenos Aires 1007
Argentina
Tel/Fax: (54) 1-327-1689

Richard Mishaan Design
Richard Mishaan
720 Fifth Avenue
New York, New York 10019
Tel: (212) 265-5588
Fax: (212) 265-6616

Richard L. Schlesinger Interiors
Richard L. Schlesinger
Lynn Gerhard
12 Pine Hill Lane
Dix Hills, New York 11746
Tel: (516) 667-3869
Fax: (516) 586-4818

Rodewig Re-decorating/Decorative
Painting and Details
Beth Rodewig
982 Broadway
Hanover, Massachusetts 02339
Tel/Fax: (617) 826-5050

Rosa May Sampaio Interior Designer
Rosa May Sampaio
R. Alemanha 691
São Paulo, São Paulo 01448010
Brazil
Tel: (55) 11-3061-2810
Fax: (55) 11-853-6689

Samuel Botero Associates, Inc.
Samuel Botero
420 East 54th Street
New York, New York 10022
Tel: (212) 935-5155
Fax: (212) 832-0714

Sandcastles, Property Design &
Development, Inc.
Sharon M. Reineke, Allied ASID
230 Nurmi Drive
Fort Lauderdale, Florida 33301
Tel: (954) 462-6894
Fax: (954) 462-6897

Shelby de Quesada Interior Design
Shelby de Quesada
1100 Sacramento Street
San Francisco, California 94108
Tel: (415) 673-2243
Fax: (415) 885-6635

Sig Bergamin Arquitetura
Sig Bergamin
Rua Cônego Eugenio Leite 163
Jardin América
São Paulo, São Paulo 05414010
Brazil
Tel: (55) 11-881-3433
Fax: (55) 11-3064-3490

Simon's Hardware & Bath
Chris Nicole Prince
421 Third Avenue
New York, New York 10016
Tel: (212) 532-9220
Fax: (212) 725-3609

Solanna
Anna Shay
1715 Newport Hills Drive West
Newport Beach, California 92660
Tel: (714) 644-8890
Fax: (714) 644-8897

Spink Inc.
William Spink, Allied ASID
66 Crosby Street
New York, New York 10012
Tel: (212) 226-8022
Fax: (212) 226-0565

Steichen Interior Design, Inc.
Laurie Steichen
1031 North Hagan Street
New Orleans, Louisiana 70119
Tel: (504) 484-6288
Fax: (504) 482-0733

Stewart Michael Design, Inc.
Stewart Silverman
Michael Cesario
420 Jericho Turnpike
Jericho, New York 11753
Tel: (516) 681-4791
Fax: (516) 681-8301

The Studio of Fine and Decorative Arts
Peter Cozzolino
Marguerite MacFarlane
101 East Palisade Avenue
Englewood, New Jersey 07631
Tel: (201) 569-9114
Fax: (201) 569-9040

SuttaDunaway, Inc.
Jula Sutta
Dan Dunaway
215 Crestview Drive
Orinda, California 94563
Tel: (510) 253-0899
Fax: (510) 253-0868

Suzanne Kasler Interiors
Suzanne Kasler Morris
2300 Peachtree Road
Atlanta, Georgia 30309
Tel: (404) 355-1035
Fax: (404) 355-1025

Teri Seidman Interiors
Teri Seidman
150 East 61st Street
New York, New York 10021
Tel: (212) 888-6551
Fax: (212) 888-8356

Thomas Jayne Studio, Inc.
Thomas Jayne
136 East 57th Street
New York, New York 10022
Tel: (212) 838-9080
Fax: (212) 838-9654

Thurston/Boyd Interior Design
Randy Boyd
Nancy Fay
801 Canyon View Drive
Laguna Beach, California 92651
Tel: (714) 376-0477
Fax: (714) 376-0479

Traditions, Ltd.
Diane Carroll
17 Seminary Avenue
Hopewell, New Jersey 08525
Tel: (609) 333-0606
Fax: (609) 333-0171

Vanderpoel Group, Ltd.
Barrie Vanderpoel
Sandra Schneider
79 East 79th Street
New York, New York 10021
Tel: (212) 472-0405
Fax: (212) 249-7714

Wagner Van Dam Design & Decoration
Ronald F. Wagner, ASID
Timothy Van Dam, ASID
853 Broadway
New York, New York 10003
Tel: (212) 674-3070
Fax: (212) 995-9861

William T. Georgis, Architect
William T. Georgis
41 Fifth Avenue
New York, New York 10003
Tel: (212) 529-5153
Fax: (212) 529-5258

Windham House
Megan de Roulet
41 Northern Boulevard
Greenvale, New York 11548
Tel: (516) 621-7722
Fax: (516) 621-0744

Window Expressions & Design
Jennifer Bardsley
83 Elm Street
Hingham, Massachusetts 02043
Tel: (617) 740-2818

Wohlberg/Levy Designs, Ltd.
Miriam Wohlberg
Pam Levy
425 East 79th Street
New York, New York 10021
Tel: (212) 734-4392
Fax: (516) 868-1422

Wylene Commander Arts & Decorations
Wylene Commander
64 East 86th Street
New York, New York 10028
Tel: (212) 744-0539
Fax: (212) 744-9878

Zeila Fachada Planejamento de
Interiores
Zeila Fachada
Rua Manuel Carlos de Figueiredo Ferraz
São Paulo, São Paulo
Brazil
Tel: (55) 11-843-4100
Fax: (55) 11-843-4652

PHOTOGRAPHERS

A.G. Photography
Anthony Gomez
27336 Padilla
Mission Viejo, California 92691
Tel: (714) 588-8569

Adela Aldama
Niceto Vega 4690
Buenos Aires 1414
Argentina
Tel: (54) 1-773-1142

Barry Halkin Interior Photography
Barry Halkin
915 Spring Garden Street
Philadelphia, Pennsylvania 19123
Tel/Fax: (215) 236-3922

Berger/Conser Photography
Robert Berger
Anne Conser
2118 Wilshire Boulevard
Santa Monica, California 90403
Tel: (310) 822-8258
Fax: (310) 822-2253

Blue Skies
Morrene Jacobs
174 Springfield Avenue
Summit, New Jersey 07901
Tel: (908) 273-4512
Fax: (908) 598-9402

Alain Brugier
Rua Emanuel Kant, 164
São Paulo, São Paulo 04536050
Brazil
Tel: (55) 11-572-6656
Fax: (55) 11-282-2299

Randl Bye
P.O. Box 170
2320 Byecroft Road
Holicong, Pennsylvania 18928
Tel: (215) 794-5459
Fax: (215) 794-0277

Cal Donnell Photography
Calvin R. Donnell
46 Catherine Street
Rochelle Park, New Jersey 07662
Tel/Fax: (201) 843-8616

Cameron Carothers Photography
Cameron Carothers
1340 Glenwood Road
Glendale, California 91201
Tel/Fax: (818) 246-1057

Charles McMillion Fine Photography
Charles McMillion
607 Brockman Center
Great Falls, Virginia 22066
Tel/Fax: (703) 406-3344

Christopher Covey Photography
Christopher Covey
1780 Vista del Mar Drive
Ventura, California 93001
Tel: (805) 648-3067
Fax: (805) 648-3197

T. Whitney Cox
143 Duane Street
New York, New York 10013
Tel/Fax: (212) 349-7894

Creative Edge Photography Studio
Patricia Rush
16320 Kopachuck Drive NW
Gig Harbor, Washington 98335
Tel: (253) 265-2238

Creative Imaging
John A. Loeb
880 Holland Road
Holland, Pennsylvania 18966
Tel/Fax: (215) 355-6356

Billy Cunningham
140 Seventh Avenue
New York, New York 10011
Tel/Fax: (212) 929-6313

David Richmond/New Orleans
David Richmond
1720 St. Charles Street
New Orleans, Louisiana 70130
Tel: (504) 529-1631

David Valenzuela Photography
David Valenzuela
1843 South Arapahoe Street
Los Angeles, California 90006
Tel: (213) 748-0644
Fax: (213) 748-7976

Dennis Krukowski Photography
Dennis Krukowski
329 East 92nd Street
New York, New York 10128
Tel: (212) 860-0912
Fax: (212) 860-0913

Dub Rogers Photography
Dub Rogers
330 Third Avenue
New York, New York 10010
Tel: (212) 696-4174
Fax: (212) 679-9760

Daniel Eifert
26 Second Avenue
New York, New York 10003
Tel: (212) 473-2562

Frank Ritter Photography
Frank Ritter
541 East 20th Street
New York, New York 10010
Tel: (212) 982-8503
Fax: (914) 831-3535

Gabberts Furniture & Design Studio
Steve Edmonds
6301 Oakmont Boulevard
Fort Worth, Texas 76132
Tel: (817) 346-5600
Fax: (817) 346-5609

George Ross Photography, Inc
George Ross
57 Union Street
Montclair, New Jersey 07042
Tel: (973) 744-5171
Fax: (973) 783-8760

David Glomb
458 1/2 North Genesee Avenue
Los Angeles, California 90036
Tel: (213) 655-4491
Fax: (213) 651-1437

Don Gormly
529 East Walnut
Long Beach, New York 11561
Tel: (516) 897-8498

Greenworld Pictures, Inc.
Mick Hales
North Richardsville Road
Carmel, New York 10512
Tel: (800) 370-8661
Fax: (914) 228-0106

Grey Crawford Photography
Grey Crawford
2924 Park Center Drive
Los Angeles, California 90068
Tel: (213) 413-4299
Fax: (214) 851-4252

Alec Hemer
81 Bedford Street
New York, New York 10014
Tel/Fax: (212) 924-7125

J. Miles Wolf Photographic Arts
708 Walnut Street
Cincinnati, Ohio 45202
Tel: (531) 381-3222
Fax: (513) 651-4995

Thibault Jeanson
c/o House Beautiful Magazine
1700 Broadway
New York, New York 10019
Tel: (212) 903-5100
Fax: (212) 765-8292

John Crum Photography
John Crum
36 East 20th Street
New York, New York 10003
Tel: (212) 460-9129
Fax: (212) 533-5644

Ken Gutmaker Architectural
Photography
Ken Gutmaker
220 Cole Street
San Francisco, California 94117
Tel: (415) 751-7300
Fax: (415) 751-4686

Barry Kinsella
1010 Andrews Road
West Palm Beach, Florida 33405
Tel: (407) 832-8736
Fax: (407) 832-0772

Kit Pyne Photography
Kit Pyne
8 Union Park Street
Boston, Massachusetts 02108
Tel: (617) 542-4898

La Chapelle Representation Ltd.
Pieter Estersohn
420 East 54th Street
New York, New York 10022
Tel: (212) 838-3170
Fax: (212) 758-6199

Bill LaFevor
1501 Gale Lane
Nashville, Tennessee 37212
Tel: (615) 297-9711

Lewis Tanner Photography
Lewis Tanner
150 West Walnut Lane
Philadelphia, Pennsylvania 19144
Tel: (215) 843-9695
Fax: (215) 843-5417

David Duncan Livingston
1036 Erica Road
Mill Valley, California 94941
Tel: (415) 383-0898
Fax: (415) 383-0897
www.davidduncanlivingston.com

Lynn Massimo Photography
Lynn Massimo
657 Fifth Avenue
Brooklyn, New York 11215
Tel/Fax: (718) 788-1774

Peter Margonelli
20 Desbrosses Street
New York, New York 10013
Tel: (212) 941-0380
Fax: (212) 334-4449

Martin Fine Photography
Martin Fine
11019 Limerick Avenue
Chatsworth, California 91311
Tel: (818) 341-7113

Mattiello/Steele Associates
20 Beekman Place
New York, New York 10022
Tel/Fax: (212) 751-8282

Kerri McCaffety
1820 Moss Street
New Orleans, Louisiana 70119
Tel: (504) 821-5025

McCavera Productions
Tom McCavera
903 Lincoln Avenue
Baldwin, New York 11510
Tel: (516) 378-5600
Fax: (516) 377-0661

Melabee M. Miller Photography
Melabee M. Miller
29 Beechwood Avenue
Hillsdale, New Jersey 07205
Tel: (908) 527-9121
Fax: (908) 521-0242

Michael E. Garland Photography
Michael E. Garland
26 Avenue 28
Venice, California 90291
Tel: (310) 827-0670
Fax: (310) 285-1580

Michael Lewis Photography
Michael Lewis
912 Tower Place
Nashville, Tennessee 37204
Tel: (615) 292-6139

James R. Morse
208 East 28th Street
New York, New York 10016
Tel: (212) 889-1550
Fax: (212) 679-3453

Oleg March Photography
Oleg March
2727 University Avenue
Bronx, New York 10468
Tel: (800) 861-3288

Rachel Olguin
509 South Huntington Avenue
Monterey Park, California 91754
Tel/Fax: (626) 280-7444

Peter Jaquith Photography
Peter Jaquith
6 Pleasant Street
Beverly, Massachusetts 91015
Tel: (508) 921-4737

Peter Paige Photography
Peter Paige
269 Parkside Road
Harrington Park, New Jersey 07640
Tel: (201) 767-3150
Fax: (201) 767-9263

Peter Peirce Photography
Peter Peirce
307 East 44th Street
New York, New York 10017
Tel/Fax: (212) 490-2646

Peter Vitale Photography
Peter Vitale
P.O. Box 2086
Santa Fe, New Mexico 87504
Tel: (505) 988-2558

Phillip H. Ennis Photography
Phillip Ennis
114 Millertown Road
Bedford, New York 10506
Tel: (914) 234-9574
Fax: (914) 234-0360

Pro Studio, Atlanta
Ronnie Owings
1602-C Lake Harbin Road
Morrow, Georgia 30260
Tel: (770) 961-4759
Fax: (770) 961-4004

Ralph Bogertman Photography
Ralph Bogertman
34 West 28th Street
New York, New York 10001
Tel: (212) 889-8871

Randall Perry Photography
Randall Perry
456 Hansen Road
Schaghticoke, New York 12154
Tel: (518) 664-2821
Fax: (518) 664-5122

João Ribeiro
Rua Cristiano Viana, 101/10
São Paulo, São Paulo 05411000
Brazil
Tel/Fax: (55) 11-881-2320

Robert Riggs Studio
Robert Riggs
332 East 84th Street
New York, New York 10028
Tel: (212) 861-5799
Fax: (212) 794-2135

Robert Thien Photography
Robert Thien
1760 Northside Drive NW
Atlanta, Georgia 30318
Tel: (404) 609-9397

Ron Ruscio Photography
Ron Ruscio
1090 Cherokee Street
Denver, Colorado 80204
Tel/Fax: (303) 685-4796

Bill Rothschild
19 Judith Lane
Wesley Hills, New York 10952
Tel: (914) 354-4576
Fax: (914) 352-8645

Sam Gray Photography
Sam Gray
23 Westwood Road
Wellesley, Massachusetts 02181
Tel: (617) 237-2711
Fax: (617) 482-1844

Samu Studios
Mark Samu
P.O. Box 165
Bayport, New York 11705
Tel: (212) 754-0415

Schilling Photography
David Schilling
18160 Briarwood
Atlanta, Georgia 30329
Tel: (404) 636-1399
Fax: (770) 582-0972

Jason Schmidt
833 Broadway
New York, New York 10003
Tel: (212) 475-2577

Scott Rothwall Photography
Scott Rothwall
273 1/2 East 19th Street
Costa Mesa, California 92627
Tel/Fax: (714) 631-5756

Studio 53
Alexander Anton
53 North Main Street
Pleasantville, New Jersey 08232
Tel/Fax: (609) 641-2934

Tim Ebert Photography
Tim Ebert
38 Oleander Drive
Northport, New York 11768
Tel/Fax: (516) 757-0887

Tim Lee Photography
Tim Lee
2 Zachary Lane
New Milford, Connecticut 06776
Tel: (860) 355-4661
Fax: (860) 350-3526

Tuca Reinés Estudio Fotografico
Tuca Reinés
Rua Emanuel Kant 58
São Paulo, São Paulo 04536050
Brazil
Tel: (55) 11-3061-9127
Fax: (55) 11-852-8735

Viewpoint Photography
Pamela Setchell
202-11 East Shore Road
Huntington, New York 11743
Tel: (516) 421-1238
Fax: (516) 421-1267

Paul Whicheloe
62 White Street
New York, New York 10013
Tel: (212) 925-1731
Fax: (212) 925-1445

Wright Communications
Leslie Wright Dow
3721 Pelham Lane
Charlotte, North Carolina 28211
Tel: (704) 366-1554
Fax: (704) 365-5523

DIRECTORY/INDEX
SHOWHOUSES & CHARITIES

ACKNOWLEDGMENTS

We would like to express our profound appreciation to all those who graciously gave their time, ideas, photographs, and support in order to help us present **SHOWHOUSES signature designer styles**.

As always, this book could not have been realized without the generous and able contributions of all our dedicated friends at PBC International, Inc. This project, which produced an unprecedented number of design submissions, demanded a heroic team effort from the onset.

We certainly are grateful to the talented designers who created the dazzling showhouse rooms, as well as to the enthusiastic members of the sponsoring organizations who helped us with our research.

A special thank you to Karol DeWulf Nickell, editor in chief of *Traditional Home*, for providing her insightful foreword.

Needless to say, our families continue to provide love, encouragement, and creative inspiration, for which we are always grateful.